Linux

The Ultimate Beginners Guide to Linux Operating System

Introduction

Linux: The Ultimate Beginners Guide to Linux Operating System is a quick-reference guide that will walk you through installation, configuration, and usage of the Linux OS.

If you are new to this operating system, this book will allow you to get complete instructions on how you can quickly use Linux on your computer, learn how to operate programs and browse the internet, and use shortcuts that will allow you to navigate through the operating system with ease.

This book is designed in such a way that you do not have to read all the chapters subsequently – you can jump from one chapter or section to another, depending on what topic you need to look up.

Here are some of the things that you can get out of this book:

- Get Linux up and running

- Master basic functions and operations

- Accomplish more advanced tasks

- Get updated regarding changes to Linux server system management

- Become acquainted with the Linux file system and processes

- Set up your network, add connections, and surf the web

- Make use of the Linux command line

Table of content

Chapter 1: Getting Linux

Since you bought this book, it is safe to assume that you have heard about Linux. Just like Windows 10 and Mac OSX, Linux is an operating system, or software that is designed to manage all resources that are associated with your desktop or laptop. However, the more important thing to answer is this: Why get Linux and learn how to navigate in a completely different environment in your computer?

Why Linux?

If you are struggling with your operating system, and you are consistently battling with the fact that you need to pay for licensing fees for every software that you have installed in your computer, the constant fear of having to lose data every now and then due to malware and viruses, and you are simply tired of your computer slowing down or crashing without reason, then you may have just stumbled on to the perfect desktop platform. Linux has now evolved into one of the most stable operating systems in the world, thanks to its continuous development by a huge network of programmers.

What makes it even better is that it does not cost you anything to install it, no matter how many computers you have at home. It is also distributed through an open source license, which means that you have the freedom to run and study the program for whatever purpose, as well as the freedom to make any changes to the program to fit your personal usage.

You will also have access to a wealth of programs that are designed to allow you to do everyday computing tasks, such as working on a document, watch or edit videos, play games, and so much more. In a nutshell, you can do everything that you do on the more common operating systems, such as Windows and Mac OS on Linux, minus the frills of having to deal with bloatware, fees, and other things that you wish licensed operating systems will get rid of.

Tip: If you are running a PC computer and you do not want to make a complete switch to Linux just yet, don't worry – you can install and operate Linux on your computer on the same PC and switch operating systems from time to time.

Can You Have Linux?

Linux can run on different types of computer systems, and because it is available on many distributions, you can choose the distribution that will allow you to install the operating system on the computer that you have available. Currently, Linux can be installed on computers with the following processors:

- Hewlett-Packard HP PA RISC

- Alpha AXPs

- Motorola 68000 family

- MIPS R5x00 R4x00

- PowerPC and PowerPC64

- 64-bit AMD64 processors

- Intel 80x86 processors

- Pentium processors

What are Linux Distributions?

When you get Linux for your computer, you are essentially getting Linux distribution. Just like other popular operating systems, you get an installation program that consists of the kernel, a graphical user interface, a desktop, and a bunch of applications that you can readily use once you installed Linux in your computer. The added bonus is that you also get the opportunity to get your hands on the source code for the kernel and the applications that you get, which allows you to tweak them the way you want them to operate in the future.

There are several available Linux distributions that you can use to date, which you can view at distrowatch.com. In this website, you can read more information about specific distributions and find website links where you can get the installation disk or download files.

While you can add desktop environments, apps, and drivers that don't come with your distribution, you will need to find the distribution that will give you the ideal setup that you have in mind. Doing so will save you the time that you may need to spend on finding apps and other programs that will work best with the Linux that you have installed, which can get in the way of setting up the system just the way you want it.

What Comes with a Distro?

1. GNU software

   Most of the tasks that you will be performing using Linux involve GNU software. These are utilities that you can access using the text terminal, or the interface that looks like a Windows command prompt where you enter commands. Some of the GNU software that you will be using are the command interpreter (also known as the bash shell) and the GNOME GUI.

   If you are a developer, you will be able to make changes to the kernel or create your own software for Linux using a C++ compiler (this already comes with the GNU software that comes with your Linux distro) and the Gnu C. You will also be using GNU software if you edit codes or textfiles using the emacs or the ed editor.

   Here are some of the most popular GNU software packages that you may encounter as you explore Linux utilities:

`autoconf`	Generates shell scripts that automatically configure source-code packages.
`automake`	Generates `Makefile.in` files for use with `autoconf`.
`bash`	The default shell (command interpreter) in Linux.
`bc`	An interactive calculator with arbitrary-precision numbers.
Binutils	A package that includes several utilities for working with binary files: `ar`, `as`, `gasp`, `gprof`, `ld`, `nm`, `objcopy`, `objdump`, `ranlib`, `readelf`, `size`, `strings`, and `strip`.
Coreutils	A package that combines three individual packages called Fileutils, Shellutils, and Textutils and implements utilities such as `chgrp`, `chmod`, `chown`, `cp`, `dd`, `df`, `dir`, `dircolors`, `du`, `install`, `ln`, `ls`, `mkdir`, `mkfifo`, `mknod`, `mv`, `rm`, `rmdir`, `sync`, `touch`, `vdir`, `basename`, `chroot`, `date`, `dirname`, `echo`, `env`, `expr`, `factor`, `false`, `groups`, `hostname`, `id`, `logname`, `nice`, `nohup`, `pathchk`, `printenv`, `printf`, `pwd`, `seq`, `sleep`, `stty`, `su`, `tee`, `test`, `true`, `tty`, `uname`, `uptime`, `users`, `who`, `whoami`, `yes`, `cut`, `join`, `nl`, `split`, `tail`, and `wc`.
`cpio`	Copies file archives to and from disk or to another part of the file system.
`diff`	Compares files, showing line-by-line changes in several different formats.
`ed`	A line-oriented text editor.
`emacs`	An extensible, customizable, full-screen text editor and computing environment.
Findutils	A package that includes the `find`, `locate`, and `xargs` utilities.
`finger`	A utility program designed to enable users on the Internet to get information about one another.
`gawk`	The GNU Project's implementation of the `awk` programming language.
`gcc`	Compilers for C, C++, Objective-C, and other languages.
`gdb`	Source-level debugger for C, C++, and Fortran.
`gdbm`	A replacement for the traditional `dbm` and `ndbm` database libraries.
`gettext`	A set of utilities that enables software maintainers to *internationalize* (make the software work with different languages such as English, French, and Spanish) a software package's user messages.
`ghostscript`	An interpreter for the PostScript and Portable Document Format (PDF) languages.

`ghostscript`	An interpreter for the PostScript and Portable Document Format (PDF) languages.
`ghostview`	An X Window System application that makes `ghostscript` accessible from the GUI, enabling users to view PostScript or PDF files in a window.
The GIMP	The GNU Image Manipulation Program, an Adobe Photoshop-like image-processing program.
`indent`	Formats C source code by indenting it in one of several different styles.
`less`	A page-by-page display program similar to `more` but with additional capabilities.
`libpng`	A library for image files in the Portable Network Graphics (PNG) format.
`m4`	An implementation of the traditional Unix macro processor.
`make`	A utility that determines which files of a large software package need to be recompiled, and issues the commands to recompile them.
`ncurses`	A package for displaying and updating text on text-only terminals.
`patch`	A GNU version of Larry Wall's program to take the output of `diff` and apply those differences to an original file to generate the modified version.
`rcs`	Revision Control System; used for version control and management of source files in software projects.
`sed`	A stream-oriented version of the `ed` text editor.
Sharutils	A package that includes `shar` (used to make shell archives out of many files) and `unshar` (to unpack these shell archives).
`tar`	A tape-archiving program that includes *multivolume support* — the capability to archive *sparse files* (files with big chunks of data that are all zeros), handle compression and decompression, and create remote archives — and other special features for incremental and full backups.
`texinfo`	A set of utilities that generates printed manuals, plain ASCII text, and online hypertext documentation (called `info`), and enables users to view and read online `info` documents.
`time`	A utility that reports the user, system, and actual time that a process uses.

2. Applications and GUIs

Since you will not want to type string after string of commands on a command terminal just for your computer to do something, youw will want to navigate and use programs in your computer using a GUI or a graphical user intergace. A GUI enables you to click on icons and pull up windows that will help you use a program easier.

Most of the distros use the K Desktop Environment (KDE), or the GNU Object Model Environment (GNOME). If you have both environments installed on your computer, you can choose which desktop will serve as the default, or you can switch between them from time to time. Both these desktops have a similar feel to Mac OS and Windows desktops. It is also worth taking note that GNOME comes with a graphical shell called Nautilus, which makes the Linux configuration, file search, and application loading easier. Should you need to use a command prompt, all you need to do is to click on the terminal window's icon on both desktop environments.

Apart from GUIs, any average computer user will also need to to use applications, or programs that you can use to perform basic computing needs. While you may not have access to the more popular programs that you may have used in a Mac or Windows computer, Linux can provide open-source alternatives that you can try out. For example, instead of having to buy Adobe Photoshop, you can try out The GIMP, which is a program that works just as great when it comes to working with images.

Linux also offers productivity software packages which fulfills the bulk of an ordinary computer user's needs. You can get office productivity apps that will allow you to do word procesing, create database, or make spreadsheets from Libreoffice.org or OpenOffice.org.

Tip: If you want to install MS applications to Linux (e.g., Microsoft office), you can use CrossOver Office. You can download this app from www.codeweavers.com/products/crossover-linux/download).

3. Networks

   Linux allows you to find everything that you need by using a network and exchange information with another computer. Linux allows you to do this by allowing you to use TCP/IP (Transmission Control Protocol/Internet Protocol), which allows you to surf the web and communicate with any server or computer out there.

4. Internet servers

   Linux supports Internet services, such as the following:

   - Email

   - News services

   - File transfer utilities

   - World wide web

   - Remote login

   Any Linux distro can offer these services, as long as there is Internet connection, and that the computer is configured to have Internet servers, a special server software that allows a Linux computer to send information to another computer. Here are common servers that you will encounter in Linux:

   - in.telnetd – allows you to log in to a different system wia the internet, with the aid of a protocol called TELNET

- sendmail – serves as a mail server which allows exchange of emails between two systems using the Simple Mail Transfer Protocol (SMTP)

- innd – allows you to view news using the Network News Transfer Protocol (NNTP), which enables you to access a news server in a store-and-forward way.

- Apache httpd – allows you to send documents to another system using the HyperText Transfer Protocol (HTTP).

- vsftpd – allows you to send a file to another computer using the filetransfer protocol (FTP)

- sshd – allows you to log-in to a computer securely using the internet, using the Secure Shell (SSH) protocol

5. Software Development

Linux is a developer's operating system, which means that it is an environment that is fit for developing software. Right out of the box, this operating system is rich with tools for software developments, such as libraries of codes for program building and a compiler. If you have background in the C language and Unix, Linux should feel like home to you.

Linux offers you the basic tools that you may have experienced using on a Unix workstation, such as Sun Microsystems, HP (Hewlett-Packard), and IBM.

6. Online documentation

After some time, you will want to look up more information about Linux without having to pull up this book. Fortunately, Linux has enough information published online that can help you in situations such as recalling a syntax for a command. To pull this information up quickly, all you need to do us to type in "man" in the command line to get the manual page for Linux commands. You can also get help from your desktop and use either the help option or icon.

Things to Consider When Choosing Distros

What is the best Linux distro (short for distribution) is for you? Here are some things that you may want to keep in mind:

1. Package managers

    One of the major factors that separate distros from one another is the package manager that they come with. Just like what you may expect, there are distros that come with features that allow them to be easier to use from the command line while you are installing the features that come with them.

    Another thing that you need to consider apart from the ease of use is the package availability that comes with distros. For example, there are certain distros that are not as popular as the others, which means that there are less apps out there that are developed to be used with certain distributions. If you are starting out on Linux, it may be a good idea to install a distro that does not only promise easy navigation from the get-go, but also a wide range of apps that you may want to install in the future.

2. Desktop environment

    You will want to have a distro that allows you to enjoy a desktop that works well with your computing needs – you will definitely want a desktop that has great customization options, and easy to find windows and menus. You will also want to ensure that your desktop have efficient resource usage, as well as great integration with the apps that you plan to use.

While it is possible for you to place another desktop environment in the future, you will still want the desktop that comes with your distro to resemble the desktop that you really want to have. This way, you will not have to spend too much effort trying to setup every app that you want to have quick access to and ensure that all your applications are able to work well as they run together.

3. Hardware Compatibility

Different distros contain different drivers in the installation package that they come from, which means that there is a recommended set of hardware for them to work seamlessly. Of course, you can check out other sources of drivers that will work best with your existing hardware, but that only creates more work when it comes to getting everything running right away from installation. To prevent this trouble, check the distro's compatibility page and see whether all your computer peripherals work fine with your Linux distribution out of the box.

4. Stability and Being Cutting Edge

Different distributions put different priorities on stability and updates to get the latest version of applications and packages. For example, the distro Debian tends to delay getting some application updates to make sure that your operating system remains stable. This may not be suitable for certain users that prefer to always get the latest version of applications and get the latest features.

Fedora, on the other hand, performs quite the opposite – it is focused on getting all your programs and features up to date and ensures that you always have the greatest and the latest wares for your Linux. However, this may happen at the expense of stability of the app, which may prompt you to roll back to the previous version.

5. Community Support

   Linux is all about the community that continuously provides support to this operating system, from documentation to troubleshooting. This means that you are likely to get the resources that you need when it comes to managing a particular distribution if it has a large community.

Great Distros to Try

Now that you know what makes a Linux distribution great and you are about to shop for the distro that you are going to install, you may want to check these distributions that may just work well for you:

1. Ubuntu

   Ubuntu is largely designed to make Linux easy to use for an average computer user, which makes it a good distribution for every beginner. This distro is simple, updates every six months, and has a Unity interface, which allows you to use features such as a dock, a store-like interface for the package manager, and a dashboard that allows you to easily find anything on the OS. Moreover, it also comes with a standard set of applications that works well with most users, such as a torrent downloader, a Firefox web browser, and an app for instant messaging. You can also expect great support from its large community.

2. Linux Mint

This distro is based on Ubuntu, but is designed to make things even easier for any user that has not used Linux in the past – it features familiar menus and is not limited to just making you use open source programs. This means that you can get programs that are standard in popular operating systems such as .mp3 support and Adobe Flash, as well as a number of proprietary drivers.

3. Debian

    If you want to be cautious and you want to see to it that you are running a bug-free and stable computer at all times, then this is probably the distro for you. Its main thrust is to make Linux a completely reliable system, but this can have some drawbacks –Debian does not prioritize getting the latest updates for applications that you have, which means that you may have to manually search for the latest release of most software that you own. The upside is that you can run Debian on numerous processor architectures and it is very likely to run on old builds.

    However, this does not mean that going with Debian is having to remain outdated – it has a lot of programs available online and in Linux repositories.

4. OpenSUSE

    OpenSUSE is a great distro that you may consider trying out because it allows you to configure your OS without having the need to deal with the command line. It usually comes with the default desktop KDE, but will also let you select between LXDE, KDE, XFCE, and GNOME as you install the distro package. It also provides you good documentation, the YaST package manager, and great support from the community.

    One of the drawbacks that you may have when using this distro is that it can consume a lot of resources, which means that it is not ideal to use on older processor models and netbooks.

5. Arch Linux

    Arch Linux is the distro for those that want to build their operating system from scratch. All that you are going to get from the installation package from the start is the command line, which you will use to get applications, desktop environment, drivers, and so on. This means that you can aim to be as minimal or as heavy in features, depending on what your needs are.

    If you want to be completely aware of what is inside your operating system, then Arch Linux is probably the best distro for you to start with. You will be forced to deal with any possible errors that you may get, which can be a great way to learn about operating Linux.

    Another thing that makes this distro special is that it uses Pacman, which is known to be a powerful package manager. Pacman comes in a rolling release, which means that you are bound to install the latest version of every package that is included – this ensures that you are bound to get cutting edge applications and features for your Linux. Apart from this package manager, you also get to enjoy the AUR (Arch User Repository), which allows you to create installable version of available programs. This means that if you want a program that is not available in Arch repositories, you can use the AUR helper to install applications and other features like normal packages.

Installing and Setup

Once you are able to choose the distribution that you prefer, you can download or the installation package or get a Live CD distribution to get Linux into your computer.

Make space in your hard drive.

If you are going to install Linux in a PC computer, you may want to shrink the partition occupied by the Windows OS in order to make room for Linux. To do this, you will need to make a partition that your computer can boot from after the setup. This is applicable to distributions that need to be installed on the hard drive, such as Debian and Fedora.

You can create a partition using Windows, or you can simply boot the distro that you have and then use the partition editor GParted. This program is capable or repartitioning NTFS drives, which are typically used by later Windows versions.

Tip: If you are going to use a distribution that uses Live CD (such as Ubuntu), you will not need to create a partition for Linux. You can simply boot from the CD, and then the installers will perform the shrinking on your Windows partition.

Warning: There is a risk of losing all data when you partition your hard drive. Before you attempt to resize any drive partitions, see to it that you have already backed up all your files.

Using Live CD and Bootable USB distributions

Many Linux distros are capable of running from a thumb drive or a Live CD and do not require you to make the commitment of having to install them in your drive. This means that you can first try out their features and even save programs in these media. However, you may find that you need more space or you want the operation to be faster the next time you boot your computer on a Linux environment. If you think that you have the distro that you want, double-click on the icon that displays Install and follow the installation wizard.

The installation wizard will typically guide you through the following processes:

1. Preparation

    This ensures that you are installing your Linux distro on
    a machine that meets its hardware requirements. You
    may also get asked if you want to include some third-
    party software, such as MP3 playback plugins, during
    this part of the installation.

2. Wireless setup

    If you want to download updates or any third-party
    software, this part will walk you through setting up your
    wireless connection.

3. Hard drive allocation

    This step will allow you to choose how you want Linux
    to be installed. You can choose to redo an installation of
    Linux, use dual booting and install Linux while another
    OS is in your computer, replace an existing OS with
    Linux, or upgrade a Linux distro that was previously
    installed.

4. Location

    This sets up your computer's location on the map. This
    is essentially helpful when it comes to communicating
    with other Linux users and interacting with the Linux
    community.

5. Keyboard layout

    This allows you to select the keyboard that you want to
    use for the OS

6. User setup

    This allows you to select your username and password.

Getting Software

Applications that run on Linux are usually available from an "app store", which may be exclusive to the distro that you have installed. This works similarly to the app centers for Google and Apple where you can find particular software and install it in your computer. For example, Ubuntu has the Ubuntu Software Center, while other distros depend on Synaptic or the GNOME. This means that downloading and installing software will depend on the distro that you have in computer.

Most of the software that you can get online are either a Debian package file (.deb) or an RPM file (.rpm). While disros such as SUSE and Fedora makes use of .rpm packages, and Debian-based distros such as Ubuntu and Xandros use .deb files, you can install both types of packages in any Linux distro. Most distros also see to it that users get GUI installers to make new software installation easier.

Installing Software Packages in Ubuntu and Debian

The easiest way to manage packages in any Debian-based distro is to use the APT (Advanced Packaging Tool). This tool allows you to make use of the apt-get command strings, which you will learn more about later.

Among the last steps in Debian installation is the source configuration for APT. Internet servers (the web and FTP) serve as APT sources where the tool will search for your desired software to install in your computer. Once you setup the APT and you have your computer hooked up to the Internet, you can get any software package by using this command in a terminal:

```
apt-get install pkgname
```

(Note: pkgname – name of the package that you want to install)

If you do not know what the package name is, you can search for it using the following command:

```
apt-cache search keyword
```

Here's an example: If you want to install a screenshot tool in your device and you think that the tool that you are searching for has the word KDE in it, you can perform a search by typing the following command in a terminal:

```
apt-cache search screenshot | grep KDE
```

This will return with the following result:

```
ksnapshot - Screenshot application for KDE
```

If this is the software that you want, you can install it by typing:

```
apt-get install ksnapshot
```

You can also get software packages using a GUI for APT if you have a Debian distro or an older version of Ubuntu. Called Synaptic Package Manager, this is more intuitive and easier to use when it comes to finding and downloading the package that you need. To get Synaptic, follow these instructions;

- For Debian

    Depending on the distro version that you have, navigate to

    Desktop -> Administration -> Dynaptic Package manager

    or

    applications -> system tools -. Synaptic Package manager

24

- For Ubuntu

  If you are using a release version that is older than 11.10, navigate to select System ->Administration->Synaptic Package Manager. If the system prompts you to enter a password, simply enter your user password.

  If you have a later Ubuntu release installed, pull up a terminal and enter this command:

  ```
  sudo apt-get install synaptic
  ```

  If you don't want to use Synaptic, you can also use the tool Software and Updates, which you can find in the Other Software tab.

Trying Out Linux

Now that you have installed Linux, it's time for you to learn navigating it. When you boot up your computer, it will go through the usual power up sequence and then proceed to the boot loader. If you choose to have two operating systems in your computer, you will have to select Linux to load the OS. If you only have Linux as your default OS, all you need to do is to wait for your computer to load the operating system.

You will usually get a login prompt after the Linux boots. All you need to do is to enter the username and the password that you have created when you were installing Linux. However, if someone installed Linux in your computer, you may see a "root" username, which also serves as the administrator account that has superuser privileges. Take note that it is not advisable to log in as the "root" user, as you may accidentally cause some changes to your system and damage your OS. If you want to perform any task that requires superuser privileges, simply type in su- in a terminal and enter your administrator password.

Chapter 2: Using the Shell

There are times that you will notice that something is not working right while you are in a GUI desktop environment – there are times wherein a program crashes and the entire system refuses to respond to mouse clicks. There are even situations wherein the GUI may not start at all. When you run into trouble, you can still tell your operating system what to do, but you will have to do it using a text screen or the shell, which serves as the command interpreter for Linux.

Since Linux is essentially a Unix program, you will be doing a lot of tasks using the text terminal. Although the desktop will be doing the job of providing you the convenience to access anything through a click of the mouse, there are several occasions wherein you need to access the terminal.

Learning how to enter commands will save you from a lot of trouble when you encounter an X Window system error, which is the program that controls all the menus and the windows that you see in your desktop GUI. To fix this error, or to prevent it from stopping you to access the program or file that you want, you can pull up a terminal and enter a command instead. In the future, you might want to keep a terminal open in your desktop since it can make you order your computer faster than having to point and click.

The Bash Shell

If you have used the MS-DOS OS in the past, then you are familiar with command.com, which serves as the command interpreter for DOS. In Linux, this is called the shell. The default shell in all the different distros, is called the bash.

Bourne-Again Shell, or bash, is capable of running any program that you have stored in your computer as an executable file. It can also run shell scripts, or a text files that are made up of Linux commands. In short, this shell serves as a command interpreter, or a program that interprets anything that you type as a command and performs what this input is supposed to do.

Pulling up the terminal window can be as simple as clicking on a monitor-looking icon on the desktop – clicking on it will lead you to a prompt. If you can't find that icon, simply search through the Main menu and select the item with has the Terminal or Console label.

Tip: You have the choice to use other shells apart from the bash, just like you have a choice in choosing desktops. You can always change the shell that you are using for your distro by entering the chsh command on the terminal.

The Shell Command

Every shell command follows this format:

```
command option1 option2 . . . optionN
```

A command line, such as a command that follows the above format, is typically followed by parameters (also known as arguments). When entering a command line, you need to enter a space to separate the main command from the options and to separate one option from another. However, if you want to use an option that contains a space in its syntax, you will need to enclose that option in quotation marks. Take a look at this example:

```
grep "Emmett Dulaney" /etc/passwd
```

The grep command allowed you to find for a particular text in a file, which is Emmett Dulaney in this case. Once you press enter, you will get the following result:

```
edulaney:x:1000:100:Emmett Dulaney:/home/edulaney:/bin/bash
```

If you want to read a particular file, you can use the "more" command. Try entering this command:

```
more /etc/passwd
```

You will be getting a result that appears like this:

```
root:x:0:0:root:/root:/bin/bash
bin:x:1:1:bin:/bin:/bin/bash
daemon:x:2:2:Daemon:/sbin:/bin/bash
lp:x:4:7:Printing daemon:/var/spool/lpd:/bin/bash
mail:x:8:12:Mailer daemon:/var/spool/clientmqueue:/bin/false
news:x:9:13:News system:/etc/news:/bin/bash
uucp:x:10:14:Unix-to-Unix Copy system:/etc/uucp:/bin/bash
. . . lines deleted . . .
```

To see all programs are running on your computer, use the "ps" command. Try entering this command on the terminal:

```
ps ax
```

The options ax (option a lists all running processes, while opion x shows the rest of the proceses) allows you to see all the processes that are available in your system, which looks like this:

```
PID TTY STAT TIME COMMAND
1 ? S 0:01 init [5]
2 ? SN 0:00 [ksoftirqd/0]
3 ? S< 0:00 [events/0]
4 ? S< 0:00 [khelper]
9 ? S< 0:00 [kthread]
22 ? S< 0:00 [kblockd/0]
58 ? S 0:00 [kapmd]
79 ? S 0:00 [pdflush]
80 ? S 0:00 [pdflush]
82 ? S< 0:00 [aio/0]
. . . lines deleted . . .
5325 ? Ss 0:00 /opt/kde3/bin/kdm
5502 ? S 0:12 /usr/X11R6/bin/X -br -nolisten tcp :0 vt7 -auth
    /var/lib/xdm/authdir/authfiles/A:0-p1AOrt
5503 ? S 0:00 -:0
6187 ? Ss 0:00 /sbin/portmap
6358 ? Ss 0:00 /bin/sh /usr/X11R6/bin/kde
6566 ? Ss 0:00 /usr/sbin/cupsd
6577 ? Ssl 0:00 /usr/sbin/nscd
. . . lines deleted . . .
```

The amount of the command-line options and their corresponding formats would depend on the actual command. These options appear like the –X, wherein X represents one character. For esampe, you can opt to use the option –l for the ls command, which will list a directory's contents. Take a look at what happens when you enter the command ls –l in the home directory for a user:

```
total 0
drwxr-xr-x 2 edulaney users 48 2014-09-08 21:11 bin
drwx------ 2 edulaney users 320 2014-09-08 21:16 Desktop
drwx------ 2 edulaney users 80 2014-09-08 21:11 Documents
drwxr-xr-x 2 edulaney users 80 2014-09-08 21:11 public_html
drwxr-xr-x 2 edulaney users 464 2014-09-17 18:21 sdump
```

If you enter a command that is too long to be contained on a single line, press the \ (backslash) key and then hit Enter. Afterwards, go on with the rest of the command on the following line. Try typing the following command and hit Enter when you type a line:

```
cat \
/etc/passwd
```

This will display all the contents inside the /ets/passwd file.

You can also string together (also known as concatenate) different short commands on one line by separating these commands with the ; (semicolon) symbol. Take a look at this command:

```
cd; ls -l; pwd
```

This command will make you jump to your user's home directory, show the contents of the directory you shanged into, and then display the name of the current directory.

Putting Together Your Shell Commands

If you are aiming to make a more sophisticated command, such as finding out whether you have a file named sbpcd in the /dev directory because you need that file for your CD drive, you can opt to combine different commands to make the entire process shorter. What you can do is that you can enter the ls /dev command to show the contents of the /dev directory and see if it contains the file that you want.

However, you may also get too many entries in the /dev directory when the command returns with the results. However, you can combine the grep command, which you have learned earlier, with the ls command and search for the exact file that you are looking for. Now, type in the following command:

```
ls /dev | grep sbpcd
```

This will show you the directory listing (result of the ls command) while the grep command searches for the string "sbpcd". The pipe (|) serves as the connection between the two separate commands that you use, wherein the first command's output is used as the input for the second one.

Chapter 3: I/O Direction

Almost all of the Linux commands that you will encounter have a common feature – they are all received from your system's standard input (your keyboard, for example), and then written to the standard output (your computer monitor). The standard error device receives any error messages that you may get. In Linux, these devices are called the following:

- stdin – standard input

- stdout – standard output

- stderror – standard error

These are also called streams, which define how inputs and outputs are distributed in a Linux environment.

Commands get the necessary input that they need from files, and in turn, they sent their outputs to another line. This entire process has a rather highfalutin name, called the I/O (input/output) redirection.

Redirecting Streams

If you want Linux to redirect the commands for these streams, you will need to enter a command that will do so. What happens is that Linux will write the output to a particular file. If the indicated file does not exist, your operating system will create a file with the name that you included in your command.

Note: If you use a command with a single bracket, the command will overwrite the contents of the existing destination.

Here is a table of the most common I/O redirection commands:

Task	Command Syntax
Send stdout to a file	command > file
Send stderr to file	command 2> file
Send stdout and stderr to file	command > file 2>&1
Read stdin from a file	command < file
Read stdin from file.in and send stdout to file.out	command < file.in > file.out
Append stdout to the end of a file	command >> file
Append stderr to the end of a file	command 2>> file
Append stdout and stderr to the end of a file	command >> file 2>&1
Read stdin from the keyboard until the character c	command <<c
Pipe stdout to command2	command | command2
Pipe stdout and stderr to command2	command 2>&1 | command2

Image source: Linux All-in-One for Dummies

When you interact with the Linux terminal, your computer recognizes your input devices, such as your mouse and keyboard, to be the ones that should be transmitting commands. The standard output and error, on the other hand, are displayed on your screen as a text displayed in a terminal.

What do you get when you manage to change the input and the output directions of your commands? Being able to do so allows you to make more complex tasks in your operating system. For example, if you are trying to manage your files or when you use Linux for software development, being able to manipulate I/O streams will allow you to become more efficient.

Getting Your Input from a File

If you need a command to take instructions from a particular file, you can instruct Linux to make use of that particular file as the standard input instead of your keyboard. For example, key in the command:

```
sort < /etc/passwd
```

Running this command will allow you to see a list of all the lines that the /etc/passwd file contains. Because you used the < sign, you have managed to redirect the standard input, making Linux think that the stdin is the /etc/passwd file instead of your keyboard.

Sending Your Command Output to Another File

If you want to have a record of a command's output and save it as a file, you need to change the stdout to a file. For example, type the following command after changing into your home directory:

```
grep typedef /usr/include/* > typedef.out
```

Using this command will allow you to search all the files that contains the text typedef, and then saves the results in a file named typedef.out. The > sign redirects the standard output into the file that you indicated. Also take note that the above command showed another bash feature: when an asterist is used, you are essentially asking Linux to include all the the files in the indicated directory, which in this case, all the files that are in the directory /usr/include.

Tip: You can append or add an output to the end of an existing file rather than having to create another file to save your output, you can use the >> sign. Take note of this format:

```
command >> filename
```

You can also change the standard out to a file by using the cat command, which will prepare small text files. For example, if you want Linux to store all the things that you are writing and only stop when you type in ZZ and press enter, you can use this command:

```
cat <<ZZ > input.txt
```

This means that your computer will be recording all the things that you are typing in your keyboard and will only stop when you press ZZ and Enter.

Saving Errors in Files

There are situations wherein you enter a command and then Linux returns with several lines of error messages. These error messages may scroll too fast that you cannot figure out what really is going on. When this happens, you have the option of saving these error messages in a file in order to know what really happened in the command by changing the standard error to a file that you can find later.

Type in the following command in a terminal:

```
find / -name COPYING -print 2> finderr
```

This will look through your entire computer system for files that are named COPYING and will then save all the error to a file named finderr. The command 2> allows you to redirect the standard error to a file.

Pipes

As mentioned in the earlier chapter, you use pipes in order to redirect one program's stream to another. This means that when you send the standard output of a program to another through a pipe, the data that the second program receives from the first will not be displayed – what you will see is the data that the second program returned.

Type this command in the terminal:

ls | less

This command will pipe the data coming from ls, and then send it to the less command. The ls command is supposed to display the contents of a directory across numerous rows. When you pipe it to the less command, the directory entries are instead placed on a different line.

Filters

Commands that change the output and the piped redirection are called filters. They are also standard commands on Linux that you can use without having to use pipes. Here are some of the filter commands that you can use on the terminal:

- grep – gives results that matches a text that corresponds to a string pattern that is sent to grep command

- tr – finds one string and then replaces it with another one

- find – displays files that has names that match arguments that are sent to the find command

- tee – redirects the standard input to one/multiple files and the standard output

- wc – counts lines, characters, and words

Chapter 4: The Linux File System

In order to find files and the directories that contain them, you need to understand how Linux tends to store them using its hierarchical file system. Despite using GUI file managers in order to find all the files and the folders that you need, you will be able to understand Linux as an operating system better when you know how it stores the data that it contains.

In this chapter, you will learn how the Linux file system works and how to use files and folders using commands.

What is the Linux File System?

Like most operating systems that you have already tried, Linux organizes all the information that it contains into files, or if they are numerous enough, directories. A directory serves as a type of a special file that is used to store other files and other directories. Because a directory is also used to store other directories, Linux is known to use a method that has a hierarchical structure when it comes to organizing files. This organization is known as the file system.

The file system allows you to have an incorporated view of the storage that is available in your computer. The file system is denoted by the root directory with the / (forward slash) symbol. The root directory contains the hierarchy of all the directories and files in your computer.

If you are used to other operating systems like Windows, you may notice that Linux does not have drive letters that indicate partitions or disk drives in your computer – all drives are all part of one unified file system. This means that you will need to know the hierarchy of directories in your computer in order to find a file that you need. Take a look at how a typical pathname looks like in Linux:

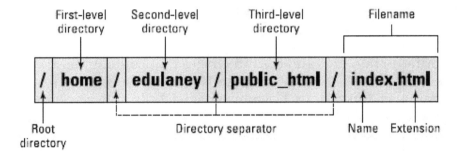

Image from: Linux All-in-One for Dummies

Just like what the name implies, the pathname is the path that leads you to a file in a file system. A pathname contains the following:

- root directory – specified by the symbol forward slash (/)

- directory hierarchy – directory names are separated by the forward slash. A forward slash is displayed after the last directory name

- filename – contains the name of the target file and the extension

The file system consists of different directories that serve different purposes. If you want to find a file, you will find it easier if you know what kind of directory will most likely contain that file. Here is the list of the top-level directories that you will find in Linux:

1. Root (/)

   All files and directories will start from this directory. Only the root user, also known as the admin, has access to this particular directory.

   Note: The /root is known as the admin user's home directory and is different from the / directory

2. User Binaries (/bin)

   This contains the most common commands that you
   will typically use in single-user modes. This directory
   also contains all the commands that different system
   users use, as well as the binary executables. Some of
   the commands that you can find here are the following:
   cp, ping, ps, and ls.

3. System Binaries (/sbin)

   Just like the /bin, this directory contains binary
   executables, but the commands that you can find here
   are used by the root user or the system administrator. If
   you need to find commands that you need for system
   maintenance, you can find them here. Commands in the
   /sbin include the following: reboot, swapon, iptables.

4. Configuration Files (/etc)

   This directory contains program configuration files, as
   well as shell scripts that are used for to start or stop a
   program. Some of the commands included here are
   /etc/logrotate.conf and /etc/resolve.conf.

5. Device files (/dev)

   This directory stores device files that include all devices
   attached to the computer such as terminal and USB
   devices. Some of the commands included here are
   /dev/usbmono and /dev/tty1.

6. Process Information (/proc)

   This directory stores information about system
   processes. This is also referred to as the pseudo-file
   system, because it does not contain any "real" file.
   Instead, it contains information about the system
   during runtime, such as hardware configuration,
   system memory, and so on. Because of this, it can be

regarded as the information and control center for the kernel.

7. Variable Files (/var)

The files whose content are expected to expand are stored in this directory. This directory includes emails, lock files, system log files, and temp files that are necessary during reboots. Its subdirectories include the following:

- /var/lib – contains data that is related to the current status of apps

- /var/cache – stores app cache data

- /var/lock – contains locked files, which ensures that a single application makes use of a single resource

- /var/mail – contains mailbox files for a specific user

- /var/run – contains data that shows system information since its startup time

- /var/lof – contains log files, which are organized into further subdirectories. For example, the subdirectory /var/log/secure contains the log for secure services such as the xinetd and sshd.

- /var/yp – contains database files for the Network Information System

8. Temporary Files (/tmp)

This directory stores all temporary files that are created during a user's session. Files that are in this directory are purged when you reboot your computer.

9. User Programs (/usr)

   This contains documentation, libraries, source codes, and binaries that second level programs require. The following are the subdirectories that you will find under this directory:

   - usr/local – stores programs that you install directly from the source.

   - /usr/bin – contains a user program's binary files

   - /usr/lib – contains libraries needed for the /usr/sbin and the /usr/bin

   - /usr/sbin – contains binary files used by system administrators

   - /usr/games – contains some Linux games

   - /usr/share – contains files that programs share with each other, such as images that are shared by multiple applications and configuration files that are used by programs by default.

10. Home Directories (/home)

    This contains all data that represents user's personal files.

11. Boot Loader Files (/boot)

    This directory contains all files that are related to the boot loader. This includes files such as grub files, kernel initrd, and vmlinux.

12. System Libraries (/lib)

    Files contained in this directory are library files that provide support to binaries found in /sbin and /bin. These filenames are typically lib*.so* or ld*.

13. Optional Add-on Applications (/opt)

This directory contains files related to add-on apps that you get from individual vendors.

14. Mount Directory (/mnt)

This directory serves as a temporary directory where soot users or system administrators can mount filesystems.

15. Removable Media Devices (/media)

This serves as the mount directory for removable media such as USB drives and CD-ROMs.

16. Service Data (/srv)

This directory contains any data that is related to server services.

How to Navigate Linux File System Using Commands

While you can use GUI file managers such as the KDE's Konqueror or GNOME's Nautilus, you will still need to learn how to navigate using the terminal, especially if you are going to navigate in a distro that does not have a GUI desktop. There are also situations wherein you may not have a graphical environment to work on during navigation, such as when you are logged in using only a text terminal. When you land in such situations, you will need to rely on commands.

Commands to Use for Navigation

When you log in as root for administrator privileges, you will instantly be in the /root home directory. For other system users, they will be routed instead to their corresponding /home directory. As a rule, you will only have the ability to save files in your user's home directory. At the same time, the user has the sole ability to create subdirectories in his home directory in order to organize files.

Linux makes it a point to support of the current directory, which means the directory wherein all files and directory commands take place. For example, you can check the current directory, which is /home, after log in by typing in the pwd command.

If you need to change the directory that you are in, you will need to type in a cd command. For example, if you want to have/usr/lib as your current directory, all you need to do is to type in this command in the terminal:

```
cd /usr/lib
```

If you want to enter the cups subdirectory in the /usr/lib directory that you are in, key in this command in the terminal:

```
cd cups
```

Tip: if you use the cd command and you do not enter any argument, you will be reverted back to the home directory. Additionally, if you use the cd.. command, your current directory will be changed to the parent directory. If you want to change back to the home directory immediately, you can add a tilde (~) to the cd command.

Commands Related to Permission and Directory Listings

At this point, you are aware that you can see items that are within a directory by using the ls command. Without any options, the ls command will display all the contents of the current directory in a multicolumn format.

However, you cannot tell whether an entry is a directory or a file without any indication when you get the results. In order to tell these items apart, you can add the −F option to the ls command, similar to this:

```
ls -F
```

This will return with more information about the types of files in the target directory, such as in the following:

```
X@ Xsession.d/ cursors/ rgb.txt xkb/
XF86Config-4 Xsession.options default-display-manager rstart/ xserver/
Xresources/ Xwrapper.config fonts/ sysconfig/ xsm/
Xsession* app-defaults/ gdm@ xinit/
```

From this example, notice that there are directory names with a slash symbol added to them. This means that they are file names that are as is. If you see the @ symbol in a particular filename, this means that the file is connected to another file, which means that it is a shortcut to the other file. If you see an asterisk added to a file, this means that file is an executable file that you can run on a shell.

You can also display more information about target files and directories by using this command:

```
ls -l
```

For example, if you use this command while you are in the /etc/x11 directory, you will see the following result:

```
total 84
lrwxrwxrwx 1 root  root 20 Jul 15 20:32 X -> /usr/bin/X11/XFree86
-rw-r--r-- 1 root  root 2878 Jul 16 14:50 XF86Config-4
drwxr-xr-x 2 root  root 4096 Jul 15 20:32 Xresources
-rwxr-xr-x 1 root  root 3456 Jun 1 01:59 Xsession
drwxr-xr-x 2 root  root 4096 Jul 15 20:34 Xsession.d

-rw-r--r-- 1 root  root 217 Jun 1 01:59 Xsession.options
-rw------- 1 root  root 771 Jul 15 20:32 Xwrapper.config
drwxr-xr-x 2 root  root 4096 Jul 15 20:35 app-defaults
. . . lines deleted . . .
```

This shows you a better amount of information about entries in this directory – at this point you can see whether the entries are a file or a directory. When you observe the line from the rightmost column, you will notice that name of the entry from the directory. You will also see when the last modifications were made, and the size of the file. The leftmost column will show the permission settings to the file, or who can read (r), write (w), or execute (x) the file.

You will notice that there is a sequence of 9 letters in the files that were displayed in the above example. Think of these nine letters in group of threes, which you can interpret as:

- Leftmost group

  This controls the *execute, read,* and *write* permissions that are granted to the owner of the file. This means that the owner can do every action to this file. If you see a hyphen, this means that the user does not have permission for a particular service. For example, if you see −rw, the user does not have the ability to run the file, but will we able to write and read it. Although all executable files allow for execution, directories tend to treat the execute permission as a function, which means that a user can execute a directory as long as he has the permission to pull up and read contents in that location.

- Middle group

  This group controls the permissions for reading, writing, and executing by any user that has access to a file group

- Rightmost group

  This group controls the permissions for any other user, including users that may have remote access through the files through the web.

This means that a file that has a permission setting of rwx------ can only be accessed by its owner. A file that has a permission setting of rwxr--r- means that it can be used only as a readable file by the rest of the world.

Another feature of the ls command is that it does not list any file that starts with a period. In order for you to see those files, you will need to append a –a option to the ls command:

ls -a

Tip: Most of the commands available in Linux are able to take options that involve single characters that have hyphen prefix. If you want to use multiple options on a single command, all you need to do is to type in the hyphen and then string together (concatenate) all the letters of the options that you want to use. For example, if you want to add the options -a and -l to the command ls, you can simply write the command as ls -al

How to Change File Permission and Ownership

There are times wherein you will need to change a particular file's permission settings in order to prevent others from reading or making any changes on it. For example, if you have a document in your computer that you want other users to read, but not edit, you will need to put some protection on the document file. The chmod command comes in handy for these situations.

In order to make full use of the chmod command, you need to make sure that you know the permission setting of the targeted file. When you have that information, you can concatenate the command with the following options in order to change the file or directory permissions:

Who	Action	Permission
u (user)	+ (add)	r (read)
g (group)	– (remove)	w (write)
o (others)	= (assign)	x (execute)
a (all)	s (set user ID)	

Image from: Linux All-in-One for Dummies

Here's an example: if you want all users, including those that are using the files through the internet, to gain a read access to files in a directory, select the letter a from the Who column. Next, use the + symbol to add the permission, and then select the letter r from the permission column. Your whole command will look like this:

```
chmod a+r *.
```

If you want all users to be able to execute a file, you can use the following command:

```
chmod a+x filename
```

Tip: If you own a file that named 'mystuff' that you want to protect in such a way that no one else will have access to it, and then you type in the following commands:

```
chmod a-rwx mystuff
chmod u+rw mystuff
```

What happens next is that the first command will remove permissions for all users, and then the second command will provide the owner of the file, which is you, permissions to read and write to the file. If you want to verify that you have entered the right settings, key in the command ls -l.

There are situations wherein you will need to make changes to ownerships in order for everything to work right in your system. Here's an example, if you want to make a directory called cups and you need to provide ownership to a user called lp with a group ID sys, you will need to log in as the root user and then use the mkdir command to create the cups directory:

```
mkdir cups
```

This will make the cups directory belonging to the user and group named root root. If you want to proceed changing the ownership, you can use the chown command as follows:

```
chown lp.sys cups
```

This will change the ownership of the directory to the user lp that has the group sys.

How to Use Commands to Work With Your Files

There are situations wherein you will want to move your files around using Linux commands. For example, if you want to copy a file to another directory, you can use the command named cp. If you want to copy a particular file to the current directory but you do not want to make changes to the filename, all you need to do is to append a period as an argument to the command. For example, if you want to copy the file named Xresources from the /etc/X11 to the directory that you are in, you can enter the following command:

```
cp /etc/X11/Xresources .
```

Now, if you want to copy all the files of a directory, which includes subdirectories and all the files in there, you can use the command cp –ar [sourcedir] [destdir]. For example, if you want all files from /etc/X11 to be copied to the current directory, you can key in the following command:

```
cp -ar /etc/X11 .
```

The command mv will be handy if you want to move files to a different location. What will happen is that the file will be removed from its original location and will appear to the destination that you specified. You can also use the mv comand if you want to change the name of a file. For example, if you want to rename the file today.list and use the filename old.list instead, you can use the following command:

```
mv today.list old.list
```

If you want to move the today.list to subdirectory in your curent directory that is named saved, you can use the following command:

```
mv today.list saved
```

Another feature of the mv command is that it has the ability to move an entire directory, including all the files in its subdirectories, to a different location. For example, if you want to organize the directory named data, which contains too many files and subdirectories, you can move that huge directory to a directory named old_data so you can rememeber to sort them later. To do so, use the following command:

```
mv data old_data
```

If you want to delete a file, you can use the rm command. To illustrate, you can remove a file named old.list by entering the following command:

```
rm old.list
```

Note: Take extra caution in using the rm command when you are logged in as a root user – you may accidentally remove important system files!

How to Work with Directories Using Commands

There will be times wherein you want to organize your directories by creating new directories that will allow you to easily file. For example, if you want to create a directory called images to contain your personal photos, you can simply type in this command:

```
mkdir images
```

After you are done creating that directory, you can change to that directory by typing in cd images in the terminal.

You can use the -p option together with the mkdir command if you want to make entire directory trees. For example, if you have the directory /usr/src and you want to create a directory tree that you want to name as /usr/src/book/java/examples/applets in order to create a hierarchy, you can key in the following command:

```
mkdir -p /usr/src/book/java/examples/applets
```

If you want to get rid of a directory in your computer, you can use the command rmdir. Take note that you can only delete directories as long as they are empty. If Linux encounters a directory that still have files in there, the command will stop.

If you want to delete an entire directory, use the rmdir command and then append it with the -p option. Here's an example:

```
rmdir -p /usr/src/book/java/examples/applets
```

Entering that command will remove the parent directories of applets.

How to Find Files Using Commands

If you want to search for files and directories, the find command will be extremely handy. For example, if you want to search for a file or directory that has the word "gnome" in the beginning, you can enter the following command:

```
find / -name "gnome*" -print
```

Take note that you may get some error messages after entering this command if you are not logged in as root. If you do not want these error messages to appear, send the error messages away by doing this modification to the command:

```
find / -name "gnome*" -print 2> /dev/null
```

Now, the above command will tell the command find to begin looking for the file that starts with "gnome" starting from the root directory, and then print out the complete pathname when it hits a match. The appended 2> /dev/null will send the error messages to a destination so that the system will not display them as you perform the command.

You can also use other variations of the command when you want to do more efficient searches in your file system. For example, if you want to find files whose names start with report, but you forgot which directory you placed them in, you can use the following command to do your search:

```
find ~ -name "report*" -print
```

When you want to find specific file types in your computer, you can append the type option to the find command. For example, if you want to display all directories that belong to the top level of your file system, the following command will do the trick:

```
find / -type d -maxdepth 1 -print
```

Tip: You can do a more efficient search if you want to find all files that match a particular string or part of a filename that you may have at the top of your head. For example, if you want to find all files or directories that you have on your computer that has the string Xresources, using the command locate Xresources will give you a result that looks like this:

```
/etc/X11/Xresources
/etc/X11/Xresources/xbase-clients
/etc/X11/Xresources/xfree86-common
```

Take note that the locate command is not installed in some Linux distributions by default. If you want to have this command in your system, pull up the the Add/Remove Software program and seach for locate. Once you have found it, select the installation package and then click on the Accept option to start installing it.

How to Mount or Unmount Drives Using Commands

If you do not have a GUI to help you and you want to access files from a DVD, you will need to use a terminal to mount a DVD's file system to a directory in Linux.

Note: Different distributions may have different mounting destinations when it comes to optical discs. For example, some distros may use the name /dev/cdrom, while others may use /dev/cdroms/cdromo. To look for this particular directory, you can check the /etc/fstab file to get the information where your distro expects optical disks to be mounted. Also take note that cdrom in Linux refers to both DVDs and CDs.

Once you have found the mounting directory, you can log in as root (or simply type in su - to get superuser privileges), insert the disc that you want the access, and then type in the following command:

```
mount /dev/hdc /media/cdrom0
```

Doing so will mount the DVD's file system on the device named /dev/hdc on the mount point (.media/cdromo) on your local file system. Once the mount command has finished doing the task, you can have access to the DVD files by looking at the /media/cdromo. This means that if you want to list the contents of the DVD, you can use the following command:

```
ls -F /media/cdrom0
```

If you are done using a mounted device, you will need to unmount the device before ejecting it. To do that, use the following command:

```
umount /dev/hdc
```

How to Check for Disk Usage

You can use the commands df and du in order to check how much disk space is being used on your computer. When you use the df command, you will get a summary of the disk space that all mounted devices use up on your computer. Here's how it will look like when you type df on the terminal:

```
Filesystem 1K-blocks Used Available Use% Mounted on
/dev/hdb6 28249372 2377292 25872080 9% /
tmpfs 383968 12 383956 1% /dev/shm
/dev/hda5 5766924 1422232 4051744 26% /ubuntu/boot
/dev/hda7 6258100 2989200 2951004 51% /debian/boot
/dev/hda9 5766924 1422232 4051744 26% /ubuntu
/dev/hda10 5766924 1872992 3600984 35% /mepis
/dev/hda11 6258100 2989200 2951004 51% /debian
/dev/hdb3 19558500 1370172 18188328 8% /xandros
/dev/hda2 16087676 10593364 5494312 66% /windows/C
/dev/hdb1 107426620 9613028 97813592 9% /windows/D
```

You will see the names of the mounted devices total amount of storage in kilobytes, the disk percentage used up, the amount of memory used, and the remaining disk space available.

If you want a more readable format for these results, you can use the command df -h instead. The terminal will return with the following results instead:

```
Filesystem Size Used Avail Use% Mounted on
/dev/hdb6 27G 2.3G 25G 9% /
tmpfs 375M 12K 375M 1% /dev/shm
/dev/hda5 5.5G 1.4G 3.9G 26% /ubuntu/boot
/dev/hda7 6.0G 2.9G 2.9G 51% /debian/boot
/dev/hda9 5.5G 1.4G 3.9G 26% /ubuntu
/dev/hda10 5.5G 1.8G 3.5G 35% /mepis
/dev/hda11 6.0G 2.9G 2.9G 51% /debian
/dev/hdb3 19G 1.4G 18G 8% /xandros
/dev/hda2 16G 11G 5.3G 66% /windows/C
/dev/hdb1 103G 9.2G 94G 9% /windows/D
```

Comparing the two results, you will see that the command df -h returns with file sizes in megabytes and gigabytes instead. Since you are more likely to encounter these terms instead, you may be able to understand and find the information that you want better in this format.

The du command, on the other hand, is more useful when you want to find out the amount of space a particular directory takes up. For example, if you want to check the amount of space that the files in the /etc/X11 take up, key in the command du /etc/X11. This will return with a result that looks like this:

```
12  /etc/X11/Xresources
36  /etc/X11/Xsession.d
272 /etc/X11/app-defaults
20  /etc/X11/cursors
12  /etc/X11/xinit
. . . lines deleted . . .
12  /etc/X11/fonts/misc
8  /etc/X11/fonts/100dpi
8  /etc/X11/fonts/75dpi
8  /etc/X11/fonts/Speedo
8  /etc/X11/fonts/Type1
48  /etc/X11/fonts
2896 /etc/X11
```

You will notice that each of the subdirectories have a number before it, which tells you the kilobytes that these directories take up. Looking at these results, you will know that the entire /etc/X11 takes up 289s KBs worth of space.

Alternatively, if you want to just want the total disk space occupied by a directory, you can append the command with the -s option instead, like the following:

```
du -s /etc/X11
2896 /etc/X11
```

As you can see, the -s option displayed the summary information for the target directory.

Tip: You can also use the -h option to read the disk information in gigabytes or megabutes. For example, if you want to see the space occupied by the home directory /home/edulaney, you can key in this command and get the following results:

```
du -sh /home/edulaney
645M /home/edulaney
```

Chapter 5: Getting to Know Linux Applications

All Linux distros come with a robust selection of applications that you can use for almost all of your daily computing needs. Almost all of these applications are easily accessible using your distro's GUI desktop.

In this chapter, you will get to know some of the most common Linux applications and learn how to access them whenever you want to. You will also get to know some of the file managers used by different GUIs, which will allow you to make changes or browse files in your computer.

Where to Get Apps?

Almost all applications used by Linux have dedicated websites in which you can find detailed information about them, including details on where and how to download them. At the same time, all distros come with different sets of utilities and apps that you can choose to install as you setup your chosen distro.

If you have a missing app in a Debian or Debian-based distro, such as Ubuntu, you can easily get that application as long as you have a high-speed internet connection. For example, if you want to find out if there is a K3b CD/DVD burner available for a Debian OS, simply key in the command apt-cache search k3b. Doing so will return a result that looks like this:

```
k3b - A sophisticated KDE cd burning application
k3b-i18n - Internationalized (i18n) files for k3b
k3blibs - The KDE cd burning application library - runtime files
k3blibs-dev - The KDE cd burning application library - development files
```

If yu want to get this app, all you need to do is to key in apt-get install k3b.

Office Tools and Applications

Average user or not, you will definitely need a calculator, presentation applications, word processor, calendars, and other staple office applications. There is an abundance of these apps available for each distro, which means that you can try them out to see which ones will suit your needs better. While these Linux apps may seem to be a little different than the apps that you are used to, you will find that you will get used to their interfaces after some sessions.

Here are some of the most commonly used office applications that are available to Linux users:

- LibreOffice Suite

  If you are used to using Microsoft Office for all your office application needs, you will find that this suite offers almost the same features. LibreOffice comes with Calc spreadsheet application, the Impress app which functions like Powerpoint, and the Writer app, which functions like Microsoft Word.

- Kontakt

  This app comes with the KDE, which is integrated with other applications such as the KOrganizer, and the KMail. This application displays everything that you may want to pull up when you enter your desktop, such as your schedule, new emails, and more. All these information are summed up in a personal information manager that is available in a graphical format.

  You can pull up Kontact by simply clicking on your desktop's panel icons or by launching it from the main menu. You can also explore all the apps that are integrated to Kontact by clicking on the icons located on the Kontact window's left pane.

- Calculators

You get a default calculator available to be used whether you are using GNOME or KDE. Both calculators are able to do scientific functions, such as trigonometry equations and getting square roots and inverses. To look for the calculator, pull up Accessories or Utilities from the main menu.

Using Multimedia Apps

Almost all Linux distros come with multimedia apps, which are mostly audio players and CD players. There are also some apps that are included that will allow you to use digital cameras or burn DVDs and CDs. If you want to play a video or a music file, you may need to download and install additional software.

Using Digital Cameras with Linux

Most of the distros available have a default application that you can use to import image files from digital cameras. Xandros and SUSE, for example, arrive with the digiKam app, which allows you to simply connect your digicam through the USB port and then import your image files from there.

digiKam functions like a typical file manager for media devices. To use it, follow these instructions:

1. Attach your camera to the USB port or serial port, and then turn the camera on.

2. Load digiKam. You can find the app under the Images or Graphics submenu. If you are loading the app for the first time, digiKam will ask you for the default location where it will store image files, plus other preferences that you may want to configure.

3. Pull up the digiKam menu, and then go to Settings->Configure digiKam.

4. Select the Cameras tab, and then choose Auto Detect. If your camera is detected and supported but the app, then you can proceed using digiKam to download your photos from your device. You will see a new window that will display all your photos.

5. Select the images that you want to save on your computer. After doing so, you can save the files in your target folder and even edit your photos with your chosen photo editor.

If digiKam cannot find your digital camera, you can still access your files using the camera storage, as long as it comes with a USB interface. All you need to do is to follow the following steps:

1. Connect the camera through the USB port

   Once the device is connected and detected, you can open the folder that contains your image files using the file manager window.

2. Select the photos that you want to save to your folder by dragging and dropping the files.

3. Close the file manager and eject the device.

How to Play Audio from a CD

All Linux distros come with default CD player apps. If you want to play music from a CD, all you need to have is a Linux-configured sound card.

In some distros, a dialog box will pop up to ask you whether you want to play the CD that you inserted in the drive or not. If you do not see this dialog box, you can find your CD player by selecting Applications->Sound and Video.

If you are using the KDE CD player, you will see the name of the CD and the current track being played. This player retrieves the album information from freedb.org, which is an

Internet-based open source database for CDs. To download the album information, you will need to be connected to the internet. However, once you are able to download this information, your computer caches the data which can be used for future sessions.

How to Play Sound Files

If you want to play any sound file, such as .mp3s, you can use either the XMMS or the Rhythmbox. Rhythmbox is one of the preferred players by users that has large .mp3 collections because it can be useful when it comes to organizing their files. You can pull up Rhythmbox by locating it from the main menu.

When you use Rhythmbox for the first time, an app assistant will prompt you to identify where your music files are stored. Doing so will allow the application to manage your music library. Afterwards, Rhythmbox will display your songs in an orderly manner.

XMMS is another option that you may have, especially if you have a music library that contains several file types, such as FLAC, .wav, or Ogg Vorbis. To run this application, simply select the app icon from the main menu. When you start XMMS, you can select a file by choosing Window-> Play File, or by hitting the L key. On the dialog box Load File, select one or multiple files that you want to load. Upon clicking the Play button, the application will play the selected file/s.

How to Burn a Disc In Linux

Most of the Linux file managers available now are capable of burning a DVD or a CD Disc. For example, the Nautilus and the Xandros file managers have built-in capability for burning discs. At the same time, different Linux distros also offer applications that will allow you to conveniently burn files in to a DVD or CD. For example, the app K3b allows you to burn discs in distros such as SUSE and Knoppix.

Applications such as K3b are easy to use – all you need to do is to gather all the files that you want to burn into a disc and then start the burning process with the app. However, take note that these applications may need command line programs, such as cdrdao and cdrecord in order to burn CDs. K3b also requires the growisofs program to be able to burn DVDs.

Graphics and Imaging Apps

Linux also offers different imaging and graphics manipulation applications. Two of the most popular apps are the following:

The GIMP

The GIMP is a program that is released under the GNU GPL (General Public License). Most of the Linux distros come with this application, but you may also have to select a package in order to install this program. The GIMP is often compared to the most popular image-manipulation applications out there, such as Adobe Photoshop and PhotoPaint.

To launch The GIMP, pull up the main menu and then select the application in the Graphics category. Once you start the program, you will see a window that will show you the license and the copyright information. Proceed with the installation by clicking on the Continue button.

Tip: If you can't locate The GIMP, add the program by going to the Add/Remove Software (found in System Settings) and install the application from there.

Installing the GIMP will create a subdirectory in your home directory, which will hold all the data that you need in order to store preferences that you make to the application. Click the Continue button in order for the app to proceed creating these directories, and then follow the instructions detailed by the wizard to finish the installation. After the installation, The GIMP will then load plugins, or modules that are designed to enhance the app's functionality. Once all plugins are loaded, you can browse on tips that will be displayed on the Tip window.

GNOME Ghostview

This application is best for viewing PDF (.pdf)and PostScript (.ps) documents or printing these document files. Ghostview allows you to view and print selected pages found on a long document, as well as magnify or zoom out on document sections. You can find this application by going to Graphics->Post Script Viewer in Fedora.

Chapter 6: Using Linux Text Editors

Even though you are capable of using a desktop that has a functional graphic interface, you will find the desire to interact with the Linux environment by editing and creating files using editors that belong outside the GUI. Learning how to use text editors will allow you to make your own shell scripts and communicate with the programs that you want to run in your operating system. At the same time, you will also be able to fix possible problems in your configuration files, especially when the X Window System fails to load.

In this chapter, you will learn how to use GUI and text mode editors, which will both allow you to configure and create text files.

How to Use GUI Text Editors

The GUI desktops KDE and GNOME comes with built-in text editors that have their own graphical user interfaces. You can load these editors from the main menu. For example, if you want to open the GUI text editor for GNOME, navigate to Applications->Text Editor and then select the file gedit. Once the editor loads, you can select the Open option found on the toolbar and then pull up a file that you want to edit or change directories that contain the file that you want in the dialog box labeled Open File.

GNOME's text editor is also capable of loading multiple files at a time and even switch in between windows to work with them. A typical editing session will look like this:

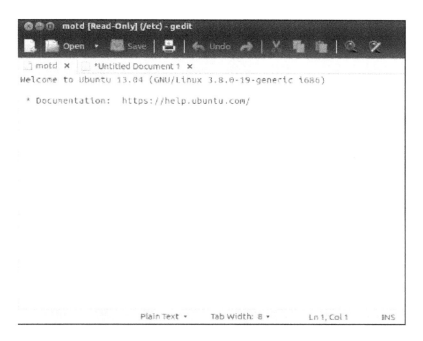

Image from: Linux All-in-One for Dummies

Looking at this image, you will notice that there are two files loaded in the editor – one appears to be a new file, and the other is named motd. You can find the names of the files that are being edited in the tabs, which you can also click to switch windows.

If you open a file that is only available to be read, you will see a text that displays "Read Only" added to the filename displayed in the window title. If you have access to superuser privileges, you can of course change the ownership of the file in order for you to make edits.

If you have a KDE desktop, you can pull up the KWrite text editor by navigating to Applications -> Accessories -> Text Editor.

Just like in the GNOME text editor, you can click on the Open icon or navigate to File -> Open in order to load the file that you want to edit. This is how the KWrite editor looks like:

Image from: Linux All-in-One for Dummies

Using ed and vi as Text Editors

As you may have noticed, text editors that have GUIs allow you to edit files using your mouse and keyboard similar to how you would type a document in a word processor. However, text mode editors are more complex than that – you only have your keyboard as you input device and you will have to type in commands in order to perform tasks such as copying, pasting, or cutting texts.

Text editors that come native with Linux are called ed and vi.

ed

This line oriented editor is going to be extremely useful when you loaded a minimal version of the OS and you do not have the support that you need yet for a full-screen editor yet. You may encounter this situation when you load up Linux from a boot disk.

Using ed allows you to work in these modes:

- Command mode – this is the default mode, in which everything that you type is being interpreted by Linux as a command. In this mode, ed has a rather simple set of commands, wherein each command is made up of one or multiple characters.

- Text input mode – this mode is for typing longer texts. You can enter this mode when you enter the commands a (meaning append), c (meaning change), or i (meaning insert). When you are done entering several lines of text, you can leave this mode by putting only a period on an empty line.

To practice using ed as an editor, perform the following commands:

```
cd
cp /etc/fstab .
```

This will copy the file /etc/fstab in your home directory. To start editing this file, key in this command;

ed -p: fstab

The editor will then respond to display this output:

```
878
:
```

From this example, the –p option allowed you to set the colon (the symbol :) as your prompt and also opened the fstab file copy that you have in your home directory. Each time the ed editor pulls up a file for editing, it displays the number of charaters that are within the editable file and then displays the colon prompt that signals you can enter your commands through the editor.

Tip: when you want to edit using ed, see to it that you have that you have turned on the prompt using the –p option. This will help you distinguish that you are in the text input mode and not in the command mode.

Once ed has opened up a file that you want to edit, you will immediately be in the last line of the file. To see what the current line number is, or the line where the command that you are going to input is going to be placed, you can use the .= command, which will appear like this:

```
:.=
9
```

From this result, you know now that the file fstab contains 9 lines. Now, if you want to see all the lines that are contained in the file, you can use the following command:

```
1,$p
```

This will return with an output that appears like this:

```
:1,$p
# This file is edited by fstab-sync - see 'man fstab-sync' for details
/dev/VolGroup00/LogVol00 / ext3 defaults 1 1
LABEL=/boot /boot ext3 defaults 1 2
/dev/devpts /dev/pts devpts gid=5,mode=620 0 0
/dev/shm /dev/shm tmpfs defaults 0 0
/dev/proc /proc proc defaults 0 0
/dev/sys /sys sysfs defaults 0 0
/dev/VolGroup00/LogVol01 swap swap defaults 0 0
/dev/scd0 /media/cdrecorder auto pamconsole,exec,noauto,managed 0 0
/dev/hdc /media/cdrom auto pamconsole,exec,noauto,managed 0 0
```

If you want to go to a line number that you want to edit (line 2, for example), simply type in the line number on the prompt. The editor will then respond by displaying that particular line:

```
/dev/VolGroup00/LogVol00 / ext3 defaults 1 1
:
```

If, for example, you want to delete a line that contains the word cdrom, all you need to do is to search for that particular string. You can do this by typing the / sign, then the string that you need to find:

```
:/cdrom
/dev/hdc /media/cdrom auto pamconsole,exec,noauto,managed 0 0
:
```

This will return with the line that contains the line that you want to edit, which becomes the current line. To delete it, simply enter d on the prompt.

To replace a specific string with a different one, the s command will be handy to use. For example, if you want to replace the string "cdrom" with "cd", enter this command:

```
:s/cdrom/cd/
:
```

To input a line in front of the line that you are currently editing, use the following command:

```
:i
(type the line you want to insert)
.(type a single period to indicate you're done)
:
```

From this point, you can enter as many lines that you want. If you are done typing, enter the period sign on an empty line to indicate that you are ending the text input mode. After doing so, you will see that ed switches back to the command mode.

If you want to save the changes that you have made to the file, enter the w command on the prompt. If you want to save the changes and exit the editor, key in wq on the prompt to perform both actions. The output will appear like this:

The editor will then save all changes that you have performed and then display the number of characters that were saved. Afterwards, Linux will exit the editor. However, if you want to exit without saving any changes that you have made to the file, key in the q command to exit without writing to the file.

Of course, there are different other commands that you can use in ed. Here is a summary of the most common commands used in the ed editor:

Command	Does the Following
!command	Executes a shell command. (For example, !pwd displays the current directory.)
$	Goes to the last line in the buffer.
%	Applies a command that follows to all lines in the buffer. (For example, %p prints all lines.)
+	Goes to the next line.
+n	Goes to the nth next line (where n is a number you designate).
,	Applies a command that follows to all lines in the buffer. (For example, , p prints all lines.) This command is similar to %.
-	Goes to the preceding line.
-n	Goes to the nth previous line (where n is a number you designate).
.	Refers to the current line in the buffer.
/text/	Searches forward for the specified text.
;	Refers to a range of lines — the current line through the last line in the buffer.
=	Prints the line number.
?text?	Searches backward for the specified text.
^	Goes to the preceding line. (See also the - command.)

^n	Goes to the nth previous line (where n is a number you designate). (See also the -n command.)
a	Appends the current line.
c	Changes the specified lines.
d	Deletes the specified lines.
i	Inserts text before the current line.
n	Goes to line number n (where n is a number you designate).
Press Enter	Displays the next line and makes that line current.
q	Quits the editor.
Q	Quits the editor without saving changes.
r file	Reads and inserts the contents of the file after the current line.
s/old/new/	Replaces an old string with a new one.
u	Undoes the last command.
W file	Appends the contents of the buffer to the end of the specified file.
w file	Saves the buffer in the specified file. (If no file is named, it saves in the default file — the file whose contents ed is currently editing.)

Image from: Linux All-in-One for Dummies

vi

The editor vi is definitely easier to use compared to ed, although it is still considered as a command line editor. The vi allows you to use a text editor in a full screen mode, which means that you can view multiple lines at the same time. It also helps to know that most of the Unix systems (this includes Linux) come with this text editor; which means that once you understand how this editor works, you will be able to modify text files in any system that is based in Unix.

Note: When you edit a text file using vi, the editor reads it into a buffer memory. This means that you can change the file in the buffer. At the same time, this editor also makes use of temporary files during an edit session, which means that no changes are made in the original file unless you save any changes that you made.

To start editing with vi, key in vi followed by the filename:

```
vi /etc/fstab
```

This will allow vi to load the file, then display the first lines of the text file in to the screen. The cursor will also be positioned on the first line:

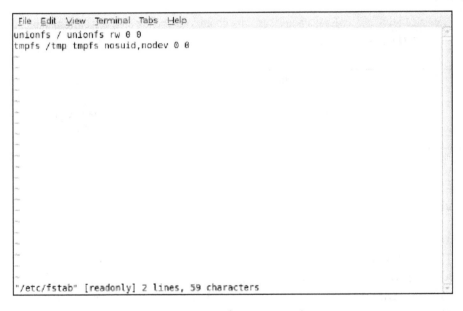

Image from: Linux All-in-One for Dummies

The last line that you see in this example shows the pathname, along with the number of lines and characters in the file. You will also notice that the file is read-only. This means that you are viewing the file as a normal user. You may have also noticed that since the number of lines does not occupy the rest of your screen, the unused lines are marked with the tilde (~) sign. The current line is marked by a black rectangle on top of the character that is being edited.

The vi editor allows you to enter the following modes:

- Visual command – this is the default mode, wherein everything that you key in is considered by Linux as a command to be applied to the current line. All vi commands are the same as ed commands.

- Colon command – this mode is set for writing or reading files, setting up options for vi, and exiting vi. As the name implies, all commands in this mode start with the colon. When you key in the colon symbol, the editor moves the cursor to the last line and then prompts you to enter the command. The editor will apply the command once you hit the Enter key.

- Text input – this is the mode that you need to use when you want to enter text into the file. You are able to enter this mode when you use the following commands:

  a – insert after cursor

  o – open a line below the current line

  A – append when at end of the line

  i – insert above cursor

Once you are done typing in your text, press Esc to exit this mode and return to visual command.

Tip: It may be a bit difficult to tell what command mode you are in when you are using the vi editor. There may be circumstances that you have typed a long line of text only to realize that you are not in the text input mode, which can be a little frustrating. If you want to see to it that you are in command mode, press Esc a couple of times.

It is also helpful to know that you can make use of the arrow keys and some keyboard to move the cursor and the screen around. Try these commands out:

Key	Moves the Cursor
↓	One line down
↑	One line up
←	One character to the left
→	One character to the right
W	One word forward
B	One word backward
Ctrl+D	Half a screen down
Ctrl+U	Half a screen up

Image from: Linux All-in-One for Dummies

You can also jump to a specific line using the colon command. For example, if you want to switch immediately to line 6, just type 6 after the colon and then hit Enter:

`: 6`

Keep in mind that when you enter the colon symbol, the vi editor will display it at the last line of the screen. After doing so, vi will consider any text that you enter as a command.

To search for a particular string, key in the / symbol and then hit Enter. The / symbol will appear at the last line, which prompts you to enter the string that you want to search for. Once it is found, vi will position the cursor at the beginning of the matching entry in a line of the text. For example, if you want to search for the string "cdrom" in the /etc/fstab file, key in:

`/cdrom`

If you wish to delete the line where the cursor is placed, type the command dd. The editor will then delete that line and then change into the next line as the current line.

If you wish to enter text at the cursor, type the command i. The editor will change its mode to become text input, which will then allow you to type in your desired text. Once you are done, hit Esc. The vi editor will revert to visual command afterwards.

Once you are done modifying the file, you can save changes that you have made by entering the :w command. To save the file and exit the editor, enter the :wq command. Alternatively, you can also perform save and exit at the same time by holding down the Shift key and then hitting Z twice.

To exit the editor without saving, enter the :q! command.

Here are other commands that are commonly used by the vi editor:

Command	Does the Following
Insert Text	
a	Inserts text after the cursor.
A	Inserts text at the end of the current line.
I	Inserts text at the beginning of the current line.
i	Inserts text before the cursor.
Delete Text	
D	Deletes up to the end of the current line.
dd	Deletes the current line.
dG	Deletes from the current line to the end of the file.
dw	Deletes from the cursor to the end of the following word.
x	Deletes the character on which the cursor rests.
Change Text	
C	Changes up to the end of the current line.
cc	Changes the current line.
J	Joins the current line with the next one.
rx	Replaces the character under the cursor with x (where x is any character).

Move Cursor	
h or ←	Moves one character to the left.
j or ↓	Moves one line down.
k or ↑	Moves one line up.
L	Moves to the end of the screen.
l or →	Moves one character to the right.
w	Moves to the beginning of the following word.
b	Moves to the beginning of the previous word.
Scroll Text	
Ctrl+D	Scrolls forward by half a screen.
Ctrl+U	Scrolls backward by half a screen.
Refresh Screen	
Ctrl+L	Redraws screen.
Cut and Paste Text	
yy	Yanks (copies) current line to an unnamed buffer.
P	Puts the yanked line above the current line.
p	Puts the yanked line below the current line.
Colon Commands	
:!command	Executes a shell command.
:q	Quits the editor.
:q!	Quits without saving changes.
:r filename	Reads the file and inserts it after the current line.
:w filename	Writes a buffer to the file.
:wq	Saves changes and exits.
Search Text	
/string	Searches forward for a string.
?string	Searches backward for a string.
Miscellaneous	
u	Undoes the last command.
Esc	Ends input mode and enters visual command mode.
U	Undoes recent changes to the current line.

Image from: Linux All-in-One for Dummies

Chapter 7: Networking

Since you are very likely to use Linux with the internet, it's only fitting that you also learn how to configure your operating system to connect to the World Wide Web. In this chapter, you will learn how to set up your internet and your Local Area Network (LAN).

Linux, like most popular operating systems, offers support for TCP/IP networking. You can use TCP/IP over several physical interfaces, such as your computer's serial ports, Ethernet cards, and parallel ports. You also use an Ethernet network for your LAN when you want to connect wirelessly to other computer systems. In this chapter, you will learn how to setup an Ethernet network and connect a LAN to the web.

What is TCP/IP?

The best way to understand TCP/IP is to think of a four-way model – each of the layers in this model performs a particular task, wherein the all layers show how data flows between physical connections in your computer and the end user.

In a four-layered model, the data makes it a point to move from one layer to another. For example, when one app sends information to another one, the data that is being sent moves through these layers in a particular order: the application is sent to the transport, and then to the network, and finally to the physical peripheral that sends it across another computer or another part of your own system. Now the receiving end gets the data that was sent across starting from the physical hardware, and then to the network, then to the transport, and finally to the intended application. Take a look at this illustration that describes that entire process:

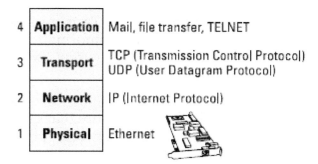

Image from: Linux All-in-One for Dummies

Now, each of the described layers possesses a set of conventions, or protocols, for formatting and handling the information that passes through them. Think about the entire process of sending a mail through postal service – the protocol that the post office follows is that the envelope needs to be addressed in a particular manner, and then other sets of protocols follow after that.

The four-layer model involves the following levels, starting from the top:

1. Application

   This runs the apps that you use, such as file transfers, email readers, file transfers. The protocols for the application level are the POP (Post Office Protocol) and the SMTP (Simple Mail Transfer Protocol) for emails, FTP (File Transfer Protocol) for file transfers, and the HTTP (HyperText Transfer Protocol) for the wen. All these protocols also have assigned port numbers, which serves as the identifier for a particular application. For example, HTTP is associated with the port 80.

2. Transport

   This sends the information from one application to the next one. The two most essential protocols in this level is the UDP (User Diagram Protocol), which takes care of sending out data, and the TCP (Transmission Control Protocol), which ensures that the information is going to be delivered.

3. Network

   This level's responsibility is to ensure that one network gets data packets from another network. If these communicating networks are too far apart from each other, the data packets are sent to one network to another one until they reach the intended destination. The most important protocol in this level is called the IP (Internet Protocol)

4. Physical

   This level refers to the hardware that is used in networking, which includes your computer's Ethernet card. Its main responsibility is to carry the packets that a network contains.

What makes the layered model special is that each of the levels described in here takes charge of their assigned tasks, and then leaves the rest for the remaining layers. The layers can also perform sending the information in a mix or match manner, meaning you can have TCP/IP network over different kinds of media and is considered modular. At the same time, TCP/IP is also supported by stable software, which makes it one of the best protocols over the Internet.

What is an IP Address?

When you are communicating with different computers on a particular network, you will need a way to identify each of the system that you are sending data to. Because of TCP/IP, you are able to determine the address of each of these computers using their IP addresses. Essentially, the IP address is based on two factors:

1. Network address – shows which network the computer can be found

2. Host address – shows a specific computer on a particular network

Together, these two addresses make up a computer's IP address, which is described by a 32-bit value. For this reason, you typically write IP addresses in a dotted decimal format, such as 8.8.8.8 or 192.168.0.1.

Internet Services and Their Port Numbers

The protocol suite TCP/IP is considered the main language of the internet worked because different standard services that allow computers to communicate with each other supports the TCP/IP. Here are some of the well-known services and their corresponding ports:

- Dynamic Host Configuration Protocol (DHCP)

  This is used to configure TCP/IP parameters on your computer. Its main purpose is to assign networking information such as domain names, name server, and dynamic IP addresses. Its port address is 67.

- Doman Name System (DNS)

  This service translates domain names into specific IP addresses. You can find this service on port 53.

- Secure Shell (SSH)

  This is the protocol used to ensure secure network services such as remote login when they are ran over an insecure network. This service is found on port 22.

- TELNET

  This service is used whenever a user on one system logs in to another via internet. With this service, a user is required to provide his legitimate user ID and its corresponding password to access the target system. By default, this service is located in port 23, but the client can connect to any system's port.

Configuring the Ethernet LAN

The Ethernet is considered to be the standard method when it comes to moving data packets between computers that are connected to a switch, hub, or router. In order to setup an Ethernet local area network (LAN), you will need to have an Ethernet card installed in every computer that you want to connect. Linux provides support to different Ethernet cards that you may choose to install.

When you install a Linux distro to a computer that has an Ethernet card, the kernel automatically detects the card and then proceeds to install the drivers for this peripheral. Your installer will also start configuring your computer's TCP/IP network. It also pays to know that every time you boot your computer, it also loads up the installed drivers for the Ethernet card. If you want to make sure that Linux successfully loaded the drivers, you can enter this command in a terminal:

```
dmesg | grep eth0
```

You may get a result that looks like this:

```
eth0: RealTek RTL8139 at 0xf0e20000, 00:0c:76:f4:38:b3, IRQ 161
eth0: Identified 8139 chip type 'RTL-8101'
eth0: link up, 100Mbps, full-duplex, lpa 0x45E1
eth0: no IPv6 routers present
```

Setting up TCP/IP Networking

When Linux sets up your computer's TCP/IP networking, the installation package also sets up all the needed files for configuration based on the information that you provide during your distro's installation. This means that you should not have to do any manual configuration when it comes to setting up your network. However, almost all Linux distros still have built-in GUIs for network device configuration just in case you need to change something.

For example, if you need to change your network's configuration, you can use the GUI which you can find in System Settings -> Network. The tool will display a dialog box that contains options that will help you change your network settings for both wired and wireless connections. If you want to temporarily disable your network, you can choose the Airplane Mode.

When you click the Options button, you will find another dialog box which contains options that will allow you to change settings for your network security and different protocols. Clicking on the General tab will allow you to select the option to always try to establish a connection and whether all users in your system can connect to the network.

Tip: You can also set your network card in such a way that it will obtain an IP address automatically. If you are using a network that does not have a DHCP server, you will need to manually add an IP address to be assigned to your network card. You may opt to use 192.168.0.0 until 192.168.225.225 as your IP addresses.

How to Connect LAN to the Internet

If you are running a LAN with different other computers, you can connect your entire network to the internet via a cable modem or a DSL. In this case, you will be able to share your modem or DSL connection with all the other devices that are connected to your network.

The easiest way to establish internet connectivity to your LAN using your modem or DSL connection is to have a NAT router that has 4 or 8 ports in its Ethernet hub. NAT, or Network Address Translation, and its router enable you to translate different IP addresses to a single IP address that will be used by your entire network. The Ethernet hub will allow you to connect your computers together as a network through the RJ-45 port. Alternatively, you can also connect your devices to the router wirelessly.

When you are able to connect your LAN to the internet, your NAT router will as a gateway, and then provide the IP addresses to all the devices connecter to it. This means that you will need to configure networking options in order to see to it that your computers are able to obtain a dynamic IP address.

Tip: Your LAN can connect computers that are running on different kinds of operating systems, as long as these systems support TCP/IP. Also remember to configure your Linux computer to automatically get DNS information and IP address.

How to Setup a Wireless Network

Your computer's PC Card manager will be able to recognize any wireless network card that is installed in your computer and will then load the right driver. Linux considers your wireless network card like an Ethernet device and will then assign it as a device. If you have an Ethernet card attached, Linux will assign this card as eth0, and the wireless network card will become eth1.

You will need to configure some parameters in order for your wireless network card to interact with a wireless access point. For example, you will need to enter the name of the wireless network, and you also need to see to it that you provide the right encryption setting. You can configure all these using a GUI that comes with your Linux distro – all you need to do is to find the Wireless Network option and enter the necessary information, which appears like this:

Linux comes with a Network Configuration tool which allows you to save all settings for your wireless network in a text file – the name of this file is based on the name of the device. For example, if your wireless network device is named eth0, then the configurations that you have made are stored in the file /etc/sysconfig/network-scripts/ifcfg-eth0. This configuration file will contain all the settings that are made to your wireless network card, which may appear like this:

```
IPV6INIT=no
USERCTL=no
PEERDNS=yes
TYPE=Wireless
DEVICE=eth1
HWADDR=00:02:2d:8c:f9:c4
BOOTPROTO=dhcp
ONBOOT=no
DHCP_HOSTNAME=
NAME=
ESSID='HOME'
CHANNEL=6
MODE=Managed
RATE=auto
```

This table will show you what these settings mean:

BOOTPROTO	The name of the protocol to use to get the IP address for the interface. The protocol used is either dhcp or bootp for an Ethernet interface.
CHANNEL	Channel number (between 1 and 14 in United States and Canada). Must be the same as that set for the wireless access point. In managed mode, you don't need to specify the channel.
DEVICE	The device name for the wireless Ethernet network interface (eth0 for the first interface, eth1 for the second, and so on).
ESSID	Extended Service Set (ESS) Identifier (ID), also known as the wireless network name. It is case-sensitive and must be the same as the name specified for the wireless access point. Provide the name within single quotes (for example, 'HOME').
HWADDR	The hardware address (also called the MAC address) of the wireless network card (six pairs of colon-separated hexa-decimal numbers; for example, 00:02:2d:8c:f9:c4). The wireless card's device driver automatically detects this address.
IPV6INIT	When set to yes, this parameter initializes IPv6 configuration for the wireless interface. Set it to no if you're not using IPv6.
MODE	The mode of operation of the wireless network card. Set to Managed for a typical network that connects through a wire-less access point.

NAME	A nickname for your wireless network. If you don't specify it, the host name is used as the nickname.
ONBOOT	Set to yes to activate the wireless interface at boot time; otherwise set to no.
PEERDNS	Set to yes to enable the interface to modify your system's /etc/resolv.conf file to use the DNS servers obtained from the DHCP server (the same server that provides the IP address for the interface). If you set this parameter to no, the /etc/resolv.conf file is left unchanged.
RATE	Bit rate for the wireless connection (set to one of the following options: 1M, 2M, 5.5M, 11M, or auto). The M means Mbps, or a million bits per second. Set to auto to use the maximum possible transmission rate.
TYPE	Set to Wireless for wireless network interface.
USERCTL	When set to yes, a user who isn't logged in as root can control the device. Set it to no so that only root can control the device.

Image from: Linux All-in-One for Dummies

If you are looking for the encryption key, you can find the corresponding key for a wireless card named eth1 in /etc/sysconfig/network-scripts/keys-eth1. If you pull up this file, you will see a key that looks like this:

```
KEY=1fdf3fdefe
```

The encryption key contains 10 or 26 hexadecimal digits. This key is carrided by

Note: If you have manually edited the parameters for your wireless Ethernet connection, key in this command in order to reload the wireless network interface once you are done editing:

```
/etc/init.d/network restart
```

To check the wireless network interface's status, type in the command iwconfig. The output will look like this:

```
lo no wireless extensions.
eth0 no wireless extensions.
sit0 no wireless extensions.
eth1 IEEE 802.11b ESSID:"HOME" Nickname:"localhost.localdomain"
Mode:Managed Frequency:2.437 GHz Access Point: 00:30:AB:06:E2:5D
Bit Rate=11 Mb/s Sensitivity:1/3
Retry limit:4 RTS thr:off Fragment thr:off
Encryption key:1FDF-3FDE-FE Security mode:open
Power Management:off
Link Quality=51/92 Signal level=-40 dBm Noise level=-91 dBm
Rx invalid nwid:0 Rx invalid crypt:0 Rx invalid frag:27
Tx excessive retries:0 Invalid misc:0 Missed beacon:0
```

Chapter 8: Making Linux More Secure

There are a lot of reasons that you need to protect your computer from other users, but the bottom line is that you do not want any user to delete or modify your system files. If you are handling a network of computers, you also do not want any user to inadvertently or purposely change anything in their system that may cause the entire system to be compromised.

As there is also a good chance that you will be connecting your Linux computer to the internet, you will need to ensure that you are always able to establish a secure connection and that you have done all the steps to protect your computer from unwanted access. In this chapter, you will learn how to create layers of security in order to prevent other users from denying you access to your computer, stealing information, or destroying your data.

Why Worry About Security

Your internet connection makes your computer an entry point for a lot of security issues, simply because you allow your system to be accessible to hundreds of millions of other computer users online. If you are an operator of an internet host that shares data to others, you definitely will want to use your computer's Internet services, such as file transfer protocol (FTP). However, these servers always have a vulnerability that criminal hackers may possibly exploit. For this reason, you will want to take extra precaution in order to lessen the risk of being attacked. At the same time, you will also want to protect your network from users outside your network, especially as you communicate with other computers through the web.

Ensuring Password Security in Linux

Unix passwords are historically stored in a file named /etc/passwd, which can be read by any user. For example, the file entry for /etc/passwd for a computer's root user may appear like this:

```
root:t6Z7NWDK1K8sU:0:0:root:/root:/bin/bash
```

You will notice that colons separte the fields in this file, with the second field displaying the user's password in an encrypted form. For the system to verify whether an entered user password is valid, the program that uses the password encrypts the entry and then compares the result with the encrypted text that was stored in the /etc/passwd file. If the entries match, then the user can use the program.

However, any hacker can easily decrypt passwords using a dictionary attack – a type of decrypting method by trying out possible combinations in an encrypted password to find out what the plain text equivalent is. If you have access to the /etc/passwd file, then you are only a few steps away from being able to crack a password. If you are not an authorized user of the computer that you are trying to hack, then you can make use of possible vulnerabilities in the target's web services, such as the FTP and mailing services, in order to infiltrate and get the file that you want.

It is a good thing that Linux has made several improvements when it comes to making the operating more secure, which include the following:

Shadow Passwords

Leaving passwords in locations that are easily accessible is bad security, even though these passwords are encrypted. For this reason, Linux no longer makes it a practice to store passwords in /etc/passwd file, which everyone can access – passwords are now stored in a shadow password file, which is named /etc/shadow, that only the root user can access.

In Linux, the /etc/passwd file looks like this:

```
root:x:0:0:root:/root:/bin/bash
```

Take note that the second field does not show an encrypted password; instead, it shows a single character x. The x in this field is your shadow password, and the true encrypted password is stored in the file /etc/shadow, which looks like this:

```
root:$1$AAAni/yN$uESHbzUpy9CgfoolBf0tS0:11077:0:99999:7:-1:-1:134540356
```

You will notice that the fields in the file are still separated by colons, wherein the first two fields represent the username and the encrypted password, respectively. The remaining fields, on the other hand, control the expiration of your password. This means that you do not need to change or even decrypt the password stored in this file. Instead, you can change the expiration date of the password using the chage command.

You can see a user's password expiration date as a root user by using the following command:

```
chage -l root
```

If you want to see to it that you will be forced to change your password at regular intervals, you can set the number of days that a password will remain valid by using the −M option. For example, if you want to force the user kdulaney to change his password every 90 days, use the following command (see to it that you are logged in as root):

```
chage -M 90 kdulaney
```

PAMs

Linux also uses another feature when it comes to improving password security by using an MD5 algorithm. What it does is that it reduces a message to a 128-bit digest, which is called fingerprint, of a document so that you will be able to attach a digital signature and encrypt it with a private key. While MD5 is known for making documents secure, the same concept works well for passwords.

Another advantage that MD5 has over traditional passwords is that you can use a longer password. As you already know, longer passwords are tougher to crack, even when the /etc/shadow file falls into the hands of a criminal hacker. You can see that the password field in this file employs an MD5 encryption:

```
root:$1$AAAni/yN$uESHbzUpy9Cgfoo1Bf0tS0:11077:0:99999:7:-1:-1:134540356
```

Another module that called the PAM (pluggable authentication module) encrypts the passwords with MD5. In Linux, you can set the PAMs in such a way that you can switch authentication while on the go, without having to change programs that are necessary in verifying identity, such as the username and the password.

The PAMs in Linux are used extensively and they are also used in different other modules in your system. All configuration files involving the PAMs are stored in the directory named etc/pam.d. To see the files in this directory, use the following command:

```
ls /etc/pam.d
```

Configuring Default Permissions

When you create a new file, who can use this file by default? You can determine the answer to this question by typing in the command umask, which will show you the user file-creation mask. When you enter this command, you will see the file-creation mask for the file that you are inquiring about. If you are a root user, the user mask is configured to 22, and for everyone else, 0002. In the following exercise, you will see how the file-creation mask works:

1. Log in as the root user and type:

   ```
   touch junkfile
   ```

   This will create a file with the name junkfile that does not have any content.

2. Enter ls -l command in order to view the permissions. You will see a line that looks like this:

   ```
   rw-r--r-- 1 root root 0 Aug 24 10:56 junkfile
   ```

   Now, you can interpret the value of the permission setting by converting the permission letters that are shown in the first field. To do that, think that the first letter gets a value of 4, the second gets 2, and the third gets 1. If you have the permission letters rw-, this translates to 4+2+0 (0 because the third letter is not available), which is equivalent to 6. Moving on to the next 3 letters, which is r--, you get the equivalent of 4. That means that the permission string of -rw-r--r—is equivalent to 644.

3. Deduct the permission setting that you got from 666 to determine the umask setting.

   666-644 is 022, which means that the permission setting is set to root.

Now, if you want to set a different umask, simply key in the command umask and then type in the numerical value of the mask. This is how you can perform this task:

1. Determine the permission settings for newly-made files.

   If you want all new files to be read and edited by the owner only, you will need to write a permission setting that appears as re-------

2. Convert the permission setting into its corresponding numerical value. You will need to assign 4 to the initial field, 2 to the next field, and 1 to the third.

   For this example, you will need to have a permission setting that is set to 600.

3. Deduct the target permission from 666 to get the value of the mask that you wish to assign.

   To achieve the 600 permission setting, compute for the mask by getting the result of 666-600. You get a value of 066.

4. Type in the umask command, followed by the value you determined.

   To get the permission setting that you want, enter this command:

   ```
   umask 066
   ```

Note: 022 is set as a default umask because it translates to read and write function is only allowed for the owner of the document, while read permission is given to everyone else. The reason for this is because Linux assumes that file owners do not want their files to be editable by everyone to prevent possible risks.

Looking Out for Permissions to Set User ID

There is a permission setting that can be seen as threatening to security, which is called setuid or suid (set user ID). This permission setting applies to files that you can run, or executable files. When the setuid/suid permission is allowed, a file is executed under the owner's user ID. In short, if the suid permission is on and the file is owned by the root user, the targeted program will view the root user to be the one running the file and not check on who ran the program in reality. This also means that the permission for suid will allow the program to do more functions than what the owner intends all the other users to perform. It also helps to take note that if the said program that contains the suid permission has some security vulnerabilities, criminal hackers can create more havoc through these programs.

To find all enabled suid permissions, you can use the find command like this:

```
find / -type f -perm +4000
```

After entering this command, you will see a list of files that appears like this example:

```
/bin/su
/bin/ping
/bin/eject
/bin/mount
/bin/ping6
/bin/umount
/opt/kde4/bin/fileshareset
/opt/kde4/bin/artswrapper
/opt/kde4/bin/kcheckpass
. . . lines deleted . . .
```

Take note that there are numerous programs that are set with a suid permission because they require it. However, you may want to check the entire list to make sure that there are no programs that have odd suid permissions. For example, you may not want to have suid programs located in your home directory.

Here is an example: typing the ls –l /bin/su will give you the following result:

```
-rwsr-xr-x 1 root root 25756 Aug 19 17:06 /bin/su
```

The character s in the permission setting alluded to the owner (appears as –rws) shows that the file /bin/su has suid

95

permission. This means that the su command, which allows any user to have superuser privileges, can be used by anyone.

Chapter 9: Introduction to Shell Scripting

Linux allows you to make use of different commands, as well as the ability to connect these commands, which has been discussed in a previous chapter. You have also learned how to make use of I/O redirection and pipes. The Bourne-Again Shell or bash, allows you to also use of the IF condition, which means that you can only run a program when you meet certain conditions. All the features of the bash can be used to create your own programs, or shell scripts. Shell scripts are known as shell command collections that perform tasks, which are then stored in a file.

In this chapter, you will learn how to create simple shell scripts that can be extremely useful in automating various tasks in Linux.

Creating Your First Script

Shell scripting, which is also called programming, can be daunting to anyone who has not tried out any programming language in the past. However, you might find learning how to program can be easy because you have already tried out different commands during the earlier chapters of this book.

If you are a system administrator, you can actually create an entire collection of custom-made scripts that will help you perform your tasks easier. For example, if there is a hard drive that is about to become full, you may want to automatically find all files that go beyond a particular size and has not been accessed by any user for a month. You may also want to create a script that will be automatically be sent to all users that own large files, so that they can be informed that they need to set up their archives and remove those files from your network's shared resources. All these tasks can actually be done with a single script.

First, you will need to use the find command to search for all
the large files in your system:

```
find / -type f -atime +30 -size +1000k -exec ls -l {} \; > /tmp/largefiles
```

Using the above command will create a file called
/tmp/largefiles, which will contain all the information that you
need about the old files that are occupying too much drive
space. Once you get the list of all these files, you can make use
of some Linux commands, such as sed, sort, and cut, to set up
and send your email message to the users who own these large
files.

Of course, you will want to not waste your time and type out
all these commands one by one. What you want to do is to do
all these tasks by creating a shell script that have these
commands. A bash script will allow you to include all these
command options, which you can refer to as $1, $2, etc. The
characters $0 is reserved for the name of the script that you
have created. Take a look at this sample bash script:

```
#!/bin/sh
echo "This script's name is: $0"
echo Argument 1: $1
echo Argument 2: $2
```

This script's first line will run the program /bin/sh, which will
then process all the remaining lines in this script. The /bin/sh
is also the Bourne shell, which is known as Unix's first shell. In
Linux, /bin/sh links to the /bin/bash, which is the bash's
executable program.

Now, save the above script with the filename simple and then
turn it into an executable file by entering this command:

```
chmod +x simple
```

Now, run the script using this command:

```
./simple
```

You will see this output:

```
This script's name is: ./simple
Argument 1:
Argument 2:
```

You will notice that the first line in the output displays the script's name. Because there is no argument in the script, the output will also not display any value for the arguments.

Now, you can run the script again, but include arguments this time:

```
./simple "This is one argument" second-argument third
```

The output will appear like this:

```
This script's name is: ./simple
Argument 1: This is one argument
Argument 2: second-argument
```

As you can see, the shell considers the entire string inside the quotation marks as a single argument. Without it, the shell will consider the spaces to separate the arguments in the command line. Because your script did not say that it also needs to print more than two arguments, the third argument is left from the output.

Shell Scripting Basics

The shell script supports features that are also present in other programming languages:

- Variables, or objects that store values. This includes built-in variables that are accessible to command line arguments.

- Use of control structures that will allow you to loop over commands

- Ability to use conditional commands

- Ability to evaluate expressions

- Ability to use functions and to call them in different places in your script.

Storing with Variables

In bash, you can define variables in this manner:

```
count=12 # note no embedded spaces allowed
```

When you have already defined the value of a variable, you can use the prefix $. For example, the variable PATH has a value of $PATH. Now, if you want to show the value for the variable count, enter:

```
echo $count
```

bash uses a few special variables when it comes to using command-line arguments. For example, the variable $* will store all arguments in the command line as a single variable, and the $? will serve as the container for the exit status when the shell executes the last command in the script.

In a bash script, you can tell the user to key in a value that you require and then use the read command to turn that into a variable's value. Take a look at this sample script:

```
echo -n "Enter value: "
read value
echo "You entered: $value"
```

When you run this script, the command read value will prompt bash to read all the things that the user enters and

100

then store that input into a variable that is named value. Take note that the –n option in this sample script is added to prevent the echo command from adding a new line at the string's end automatically.

Calling Functions

You can lump together a group of commands into a function with an assigned name, and then use them during different areas in your script. Once you have commands grouped into a function, you can simply key in the function's name to execute all the commands that was assigned to it. Take a look at this sample script:

```
#!/bin/sh
hello() {
echo -n "Hello, "
echo $1 $2
}
hello Jane Doe
```

Running this script will give you this output:

```
Hello, Jane Doe
```

This script defined the function which was named hello. You will notice that the second line of the script displays hello (), which means that the function is being defined as such, and that the body of the function which tells you the commands included in the function is enclosed within curly braces. In this example, the body of the function made use of two echo commands to display a string and two arguments.

Controlling the Scrip Flow

You can have control of how the script will execute the commands that you have indicated by using special commands. Commands like *if, while, case,* and *for* allows you to use a command's exit status and then do the next action. When a command is executed, it gives an exit status, or a numerical value that indicates whether you have succeeded in executing the command. By programming convention, having an exit status of zero means that the command has been accomplished.

For example, you want to make a copy of a file before you pull up the vi editor to make some changes to the file. At the same time you also want to make it a point that no changes are going to be made to the file if the backup file is not created. To take care of all these tasks, you can use the following script:

```
#!/bin/sh
if cp "$1" "#$1"
then
vi "$1"
else
echo "Failed to create backup copy"
fi
```

This script shows the syntax of the structure if-then-else and also displays how the cp command's exit status by the if command, which determines what the next action is going to be. If the cp displays an exit status of zero, you will have access to vi to edit the file. If that is not the case, the script will show you an error message and then exits. Also take note that the script will save the backup file that you have requested using the same filename, but with a hashtag at the beginning of the backup file's name.

Also take note that you need to enter the command fi to let the script know that you have ended the if command. Otherwise, you will encounter an error in your script.

If you want to evaluate any expression and also use the value of the expression to serve as a command's exit status, the test command is going to be handy for that task. For example, if you want to create a script that will only edit an existing file, you can use the test command in this manner:

```
#!/bin/sh
if test -f "$1"
then
vi "$1"
else
echo "No such file"
fi
```

Take note that you can also use a shorter test command by using the square bracket ([ ]) to contain the expression. You can edit the above sample script to look like this:

```
#!/bin/sh
if [ -f "$1" ]
then
vi "$1"
else
echo "No such file"
fi
```

Another control structure that you can use is the for loop. Take a look at how this control structure is used in this script that is designed to add the numbers 1 through 10:

```
#!/bin/sh
sum=0
for i in 1 2 3 4 5 6 7 8 9 10
do
sum='expr $sum + $i'
done
echo "Sum = $sum"
```

Take note that the above script also showed how the expr command was used to evaluate an expression.

If you want to execute a command group according to variable value, the case statement is going to be useful. Take a look at this example script:

```
#!/bin/sh
echo -n "What should I do -- (Y)es/(N)o/(C)ontinue? [Y] "
read answer
case $answer in
y|Y|"")
echo "YES"
;;
c|C)
echo "CONTINUE"
;;
n|N)
echo "NO"
;;
*)
echo "UNKNOWN"
;;
esac
```

Now, save this script as confirm, and then enter this command to turn it into an executable file:

chmod +x confirm

When the script prompts you for a requested action, press any of these keys: Y, N, or C. This is how the output will look like:

```
What should I do -- (Y)es/(N)o/(C)ontinue? [Y] c
CONTINUE
```

The script stores your input into the variable answer, and the case statement runs a code according to the value of your input. For example, if you press the C key, this code block will run:

```
c|C)
echo "CONTINUE"
;;
```

As the code's output, the text CONTINUE is displayed.

Take a look at another example to see how the case command's syntax is used:

```
case $variable in
value1 | value2)
command1
command2
. . . other commands . . .
;;
value3)
command3
command4
. . . other commands . . .
;;
esac
```

You will notice that the case command starts with the word case and then terminates with the word esac. There are also code blocks that are contained within the variable values, which were followed by a closing parenthesis. When all other commands for the script are already entered, they are ended with two semicolons.

Conclusion

Thank you for reading this book! I hope that this book has helped you learn how to use Linux confidently, from installing it into your computer to creating your own programs using this operating system.

I also hope that this book has served as a guide in choosing the best Linux distribution for your needs, as well as applications that will help you perform daily computing tasks. By the end of this book, you should have also learned how to operate within Linux environment using the command line and have managed to learn some steps in making your system secure.

The next step is to learn more about creating and editing shell scripts and create automation scripts that will allow you to use Linux in a more efficient manner.

Finally, if you have enjoyed reading this book, please take the time to encourage your friends and family to get their own copy. I will also appreciate it if you can tell other readers what you think about this book on Amazon.com. I am looking forward to hear from you soon!

Bonus: Preview Of Python: The Ultimate Beginners Guide

In this generation of computer programming and highly technical applications, it's smart to move with the times. If you don't, you will be left behind in many undertakings that you want to pursue.

If you want to be the cream of the crop, you must learn how to create and read computer or programming language. Your knowledge will not only set you apart from your contemporaries, but will also boost your productivity and self-advancement in relevance with the expanding world of computer lingo.

What is Python?

Python is a powerful programming language. You can use it for free in developing software that can run on Nokia mobile phones, Windows, Mac OS X, Linux, Unix, JAVA, Amiga, and many more operating systems.

Python is object-oriented and provides simple and easy to read and use language that you can utilize in creating your programs.

Even if you're not a programmer, it would be beneficial for you to know about Python because of the numerous uses you can take advantage of.

So, where is Python used?

Here is a summary of the uses of Python:

1. To process images
2. To write Internet scripts
3. To embed scripts

4. To manipulate database programs
5. To provide system utilities
6. To create artificial intelligence
7. To create graphical user interface applications using IDEs on Windows and other platforms

Advantages of learning Python

For you to understand more what you stand to gain from learning Python, here are its major pros.

You can:

1. Learn Python easily because the syntax or language in programming is simple.
2. Prepare codes readily that can be used in various operating systems such as Linux, Windows, Unix and Mac OS X.
3. Promptly access the Python standard library that helps users in creating, editing, accessing, running and maintaining files.
4. Integrate programs and systems promptly because the programming language is easy to follow.
5. Handle the errors more reliably because the syntax is capable of identifying and raising exceptions.
6. Learn more quickly because the programming language is object oriented.
7. Access IDLE, which makes it possible for users to create codes and check if the codes work, through Python's interactive system.
8. Download Python for free, and enjoy all the benefits of a free application.
9. Embed your Python data in other systems.
10. Stop worrying about freeing the memory for your codes, because Python does it automatically.

If you're in, then, let's start the ball rolling!

www.ingramcontent.com/pod-product-compliance
Lightning Source LLC
Chambersburg PA
CBHW071006050326
40689CB00014B/3506